CROSS COLORS

American Christianity in Black and White

HAMAN CROSS, JR.

Cross Colors: American Christianity in Black and White
© 2015 by Haman Cross, Jr.

All rights reserved. No part of this book may be used or reproduced by any means, graphic, electronic, or mechanical, including photocopying, recording, taping or by any information storage retrieval system without the written permission of the author except in the case of brief quotations embodied in critical articles and reviews.

Scripture quotations, unless otherwise indicated, are taken from the Holy Bible, New International Version®, NIV®. Copyright ©1973, 1978, 1984, 2011 by Biblica, Inc.™ Used by permission of Zondervan. All rights reserved worldwide. www.zondervan.com The "NIV" and "New International Version" are trademarks registered in the United States Patent and Trademark Office by Biblica, Inc.™

Scripture quotations marked NLT are taken from the Holy Bible, New Living Translation. © 1996. Used by permission of Tyndale House Publishers, Inc., Wheaton, Ill. 60189. All rights reserved.

Scripture quotations marked KJV are from the King James Version.

Scripture quotations marked NKJV are from the New King James Version. © 1982, 1992 by Thomas Nelson, Inc. Used by permission. All rights reserved.

Scripture quotations marked NJB are from The New Jerusalem Bible, copyright © 1985 by Darton, Longman & Todd, Ltd. and Doubleday, a division of Random House, Inc. Reprinted by Permission.

ISBN 978-0-692-43423-9

Second Printing, July 2015. Printed in the U.S.A.

www.CrossColorsWithMe.com

Acknowledgements

The following people deserve my deepest gratitude for helping me Cross Colors during my lifetime and while working on this book:

Rosedale Park Baptist Church Family
Mr. Roger Johnson & Dr. Jerrolynn Hockenhull-Johnson
Dr. Gerry Koning, Trinity Christian Reformed Church
Ms. Amanda Johnson
Dr. Matthew Parker, Institute for Black Family Development
Pastor Charles Lyons, Armitage Baptist Church
Dr. Willie Richardson, Christian Stronghold Baptist Church
And last but certainly not least, my Cross Clan.

Eternally Grateful,

Haman Cross, Jr.

Table of Contents

Prologue	6
1. The Ideal African American Church	10
2. Cross Colors	21
3. Manna: What is It?	25
4. Walls (Brick and Mortar)	40
5. Walls (Revisited)	49
6. How it All Began	54
7. Finding Out the Truth	60
8. Walls Against Authority and Walls of Self-Rejection	71
9. Stew Pot or Melting Pot?	90
10. Tough Talk	96
11. Partiality and Evangelism Make Strange Bedfellows	116
12. What We Believe (Really)	133
13. How Did Haman Cross the Divide?	137
14. How Did Haman Cross the Divide (v. 2.0)?	145
15. A Tale of Two Churches	155
16. The Ideal African American Church	160
Epilogue	162

Prologue

"The only thing necessary for the triumph of evil is for good men to do nothing."
- Edmund Burke

Let go of the knife!
Oh my God! Please don't let him get hurt! PLEASE!
When my oldest child, Haman Cross III, was three years old, my wife, Roberta, and I carelessly left a razor-sharp butcher's knife on the kitchen table. This was back before the term "child-proofing" one's house became an integral part of the nation's vocabulary. Imagine our surprise and horror when our three-year-old son came toddling into the living room carrying the huge, sharp knife! I literally felt my heart stop.

Pictures—bloody, horrible pictures—flashed through my mind.

My son drops the knife and it sticks into his foot...

My child grabs the blade with his free hand, opening a gash in it...

Haman III decides to run toward Roberta and me to show off the new toy he has just found, trips, falls, and...

I immediately dropped to my knees to reason with him eye-to-eye.

"Haman, give Dad the knife."

He looked at me, a big smile spreading across his chubby little face, squeezing the handle of the knife in his pudgy little hand, and said—triumphantly—what most three year olds say, "NO! MINE!"

I pleaded with him. *"Come on, Haman. Give Dad the knife."*

"NO! MINE!"

I was big-time scared. Too scared to try to raise my voice and use an adult's last line of defense with a child—intimidation—to get him to drop the knife.

Too scared to step toward him, since he would probably run away from me, trip, fall, and...

The point of the knife...

I shook that image out of my head and continued to plead with him. I knew this was a life or death situation, but it was all such a game to him. The knife was no different from the teddy bears and balls that he picked up around the house, telling anyone who bothered to ask him for it, "NO! MINE!"

This was just something that he decided he wanted, never mind that I was asking him to put it down. Never mind that it was a weapon that I—his father—knew could injure or even kill him. In his mind this was his, and he had a right to it. He didn't realize how high the stakes were or the life-long, potentially life-threatening consequences. He was just a child after all.

"Please, son. Give me the knife."

"NO! MINE!"

"Haman, put down the knife."

Scenarios began racing through my mind faster now, and with greater urgency.

He's not that far away from me. If I move quickly enough, I can probably get it away from him. A quick snatch and...

He grabs the blade and loses a few fingers...

But losing a few fingers is better than his losing his life. If I wasn't quick enough though, I might lose a few fingers! That was still better than his being hurt.

I could just reach out and grab him, and maybe shake him loose from the knife. He moves a little quicker than I do, he thinks I'm playing with him, starts to run... trips... falls...and...

If he only knew how dangerous his new "toy" was. What do I do?

"Son, please let go of the knife."

My thoughts raced, "GOD PLEASE HELP ME. HELPME. HELPME. HELPME! I don't want my child to get hurt. Please get him to drop it. If I try to do something, he might hurt himself. PLEASE GET HIM TO LET GO OF THE KNIFE."

"PLEASE son. Let go of the knife."

Reflecting back on this incident with my son has helped me to see that God goes through the same thing with us, His children. We, too, are holding a sharp knife that we don't want to, or can't, recognize as life-threateningly dangerous. But God knows that it is, and He is pleading with His Church—His Children—in America:

"PLEASE LET GO. LET GO OF THE KNIFE."

"PLEASE LET GO OF THE KNIFE OF PARTIALITY AND RACISM."

Many Christians in America have no doubt that partiality is a problem in our country and throughout the world. America and its citizens have suffered from it and its repercussions almost from its inception. Yet complacency, misunderstanding, ignorance, and/or fear about doing anything substantive about it, let alone change it, paralyzes us.

The Church should be leading the way with feasible solutions to this dangerous situation, but where, oh where, is that leadership? It seems that many of us would rather ignore it and deal with other, more pressing issues.

Do we really understand that partiality among the people of God is deadly to God's purposes on this earth? Does the Church in America know that without addressing and solving this issue it will never move in the direction that God wants? Do we have a clear understanding that, without winning this war—not just a battle but the war—the Church in America cannot and will not glorify God; cannot and will not live up to its potential and thereby will be looked at as a mockery and its members hypocrites?

Are we preparing to win this war? Are we ready to do the work to win this war? Are we willing to let go of the knife? Are we willing to cross the color lines? Is it really worth it? Do we really care?

As Christians, the answer to these questions must be a resounding, "Yes! Yes, Lord! Yes! I care! Now!"

I haven't always felt this way, however. I haven't always wanted to *Cross Colors*. For a long time I didn't realize I was playing with a deadly weapon, and because of my ignorance, anger and fear I wouldn't let go of the knife. But God told me, and through his Word showed me, how to let go of the knife forever. I'll be the first to admit that this has not been an easy process, but it has been a process filled to overflowing with the grace of God.

Are you a Christian who is openly holding on to the knife of partiality? Or are you one of those Christians who have put the knife in your back pocket, not sure if you should really let go of it for good or not? Are you a Christian who has decided that because you aren't holding that knife the problem is going to go away, or has gone away? If you are one of these Christians, I'm here to tell you a few very important things.

First, the knife of partiality is not safe to handle any longer (and ultimately has never been).

Second, you need to know that it is not going to go away just because you are ignoring it.

Finally, it is time to face the fact that God absolutely wants you to let it go. I've written this book to help you let go by sharing my journey.

I am certain that as a result of reading this book, you will be motivated to let go of the knife of partiality, trust in God, and do this *Cross Colors* thing.

1

The Ideal African American Church

"The church must face its historic obligation because the segregation problem is more of a moral problem than a political problem."
- Rev. Dr. Martin Luther King, Jr.
("Stride Toward Freedom")

Several years ago, I started a church in Detroit. The goal was to begin an African American middle-class church. This was to be a black church that would do some progressive things, not just have car washes, sell rib dinners or build a new edifice on the storefront that we bought.

This church would attract African Americans as diverse as the very color of our own complexions. I planned that every ministry included in the church would mirror this progressive spirit. Even our music ministry would be extraordinary. Our congregation contained classical, jazz and contemporary musicians and I planned for our services to be as diverse and eclectic as we were. We would be *different*.

This idea was well-defined and outlined in our mission statement: "The Up and Outers, reaching the Down and Outers." The vision was that people—black people—who had once lived in the city, received an education and accomplished personal and financial gains, would give back to their community—the black community—through our church. As the founding pastor, I was fired up, excited, and pleased about it all. I made it very clear to the Lord and the congregation that there wouldn't be any righteous thing that we would be unwilling to do in fulfilling this vision. We would be "The Ideal African American Church."

I targeted the black middle and upper middle class communities for my membership and determined that our finances would come from this same group.

This was very important to me. I was the son of a pastor and I desperately wanted to do things differently from my father. My father had worked with poor black families for years. I wanted to move into another realm, and I wanted to deal with the black middle and upper classes. I knew that it would be a completely different landscape from the one I had been intimately involved with through my father's ministry.

Our family was from the black lower class. Most of the time, my father had to solicit money from whites to fund his ministry. I absolutely did not want to do that! I wanted the black middle and upper classes to do something on their own. I did not want to beg for money from whites. I determined from the beginning that I didn't need or want their handouts or help. I reassured myself that I wasn't a bigot or anything like that. I just did not want "them" involved with my church.

Then, I spent a great deal of time traveling to college campuses around the country. Many times, I found myself preaching and teaching to predominantly white audiences. That was cool. I could deal with that. It was just that when I came home—to *my* church—I didn't want to have to deal with them.

They have their concerns and issues, and we have ours. Who after all would be better suited for pastoring, preaching, and teaching inner-city African Americans than other African Americans? I didn't even want to ask them for financial support because then I might have to listen to their input. Better to just let everyone take care of his or her own. Like I said, I wasn't a bigot or anything; I just felt my church should be filled with African American people on Sunday.

I began the church. Things went exactly as I had planned—Up and Outers reaching the Down and Outers. I did my best to let the Holy Spirit work in and through me to fulfill the vision that my congregation and I had for our church, and for five years our church grew. I would look out at my congregation from the pulpit every Sunday morning and every Wednesday night and think of how wonderful it was to live out this dream.

I especially loved this view on Sunday mornings. One Sunday, I was reveling in the Spirit and the beauty of my congregation; appreciating the African American brothers and sisters and their children and all the different shades we can have: cream colored, dark chocolate, milk chocolate, ebony and ivory.

IVORY!?!

What the...? There was a white person sitting in my church! Wait, not just a white person. It looked like they had brought their entire family! I couldn't believe it—a white family sitting in my church! Who let them in? Why were they here? We didn't invite them, but they came anyway! Where did they come from?

Whenever I would speak throughout the week at conferences and seminars, white folks would approach me afterward to talk and shake hands. I heard every week from different white folks of how if they lived in Detroit, I would be the kind of preacher that they wanted as their pastor. I would nod, smile and tell them to "please come." But, in my mind I knew that they were just talking and grinning in my face like so many others had done in the past.

"I really loved that message, Pastor Cross."

Smile.

"Come back and hear the rest of the series."

"You brought up some very good points in your sermon. You are exactly the kind of preacher I need."

Nod.

"Thank you."

"If you had a church here I'd be one of your first members."

Smile. Handshake.

"Thanks for the compliment."

"The next time I'm around Detroit I'm going to visit your church."

Nod. Smile. Handshake.

"Please do. You're always welcome."

They would say things like that and I would respond accordingly. Coming and joining my church though? I knew that they had no real intention of doing anything like that. We would be nodding, smiling and lying to each other, because we both knew that those are the things that black Christians and white Christians say to each other when we are at conferences together. We would say those kinds to each other, knowing that every Sunday we gathered in our own houses of worship.

I looked out at these white folks sitting in my church and couldn't believe it.

What do they want? Visitors! That's who they are! They're probably visitors, from out of town. Probably somebody that attended a conference where I spoke was in town for a weekend and wanted to come in and get a black church experience. Yeah that's who they probably are.

Like I said, I'm *not* a bigot.

They were visiting, so I didn't want them to feel like I had felt so many times at white churches when I was the only black person. I didn't want them to feel as if every eye in the church, including the pastor's, was on them.

After the initial shock, I was okay with it. It was fine for them to visit. I was cool with it, really. They were welcome to come to Sunday services. They could drive by the church and walk through the facility. I didn't have a problem with that. Like I said, I wasn't a bigot or anything.

But you know, they should really try looking into another church. One better suited for their needs.

The next week they were back again, and the week after that and the week after that.

When I mentioned it to a few friends who weren't pastors, they asked, "So, what you gonna do, Cross? You gonna start singing 'The Old Rugged Cross' like you in the opera or sumthin'?"

"No, I ain't even gonna' go there. I just wish they would chill out on the visiting, because they are really messin' up my thang."

I got my wish. They finally chilled out on the visiting.

One Sunday morning, the white family that had been visiting responded to the invitation to join my black, middle class, church.

What's up with this? What's going on here?

Then another white family joined.

Hold up!

Then another.

Wait a minute!

I was totally blown away. These people completely changed the complexion of our church.

Hey, this was NOT in our mission statement!

This was, after all, Detroit, Michigan, one of the most segregated cities in the country. For the most part in and around Detroit, you either went to an all-black church or an all-white church. This was what I had been seeing my entire life in this city.

When white people started coming to Rosedale Park Baptist Church, it cramped my style. I could no longer say ours was a black middle class church. We now had white people in our church. I now had to be sensitive to whites. I had to change the way I preached. Some of the references had to be explained so that they understood. Some of my references had to be completely thrown out so that I wouldn't offend them. I had to make sure that my messages wouldn't alienate these white people.

I wanted the Ideal African American Church. Both the Up and Outers and the Down and Outers that I had had in mind were supposed to be black. My staff was afro-centric. I wanted our church to have an afro-centric identity. These white folks were forcing us all—us black folks—to make adjustments. We had all types of programs in motion and in development that were specifically aimed at the uplifting and empowerment of African Americans. I hated having to make adjustments for them.

I'm sick and tired of adjusting to them. Haven't we been adjusting to them FOREVER? Maybe I shouldn't change a thing and let them adjust and adapt to us for once. I should do a sermon series on how white folks want us to hate ourselves. That's why they've got all these pictures of a blond blue-eyed Jesus hanging everywhere. I wonder how many of them would sit through that? I could do that and let them feel what we go through ALL THE TIME! If it made them uncomfortable, that was something that couldn't be helped. They would just have to deal with it. Yeah, they would just have to deal with it or leave.

I was cool with both of those possibilities. I wanted to please my staff, my church, and myself. Frankly, I just did not want to deal with this situation.

And to make matters worse, these white folks who had joined my church (I wasn't able to call them "members" of my church just yet) started asking me things like:

"Will there be any music we can relate to?"

WHAT!?! Music that you can relate to? What's wrong with the music we're playing?

"Will there be programs uniquely for us?"

No. I don't think we'll be performing Handel's Messiah just yet.

"I'm interested in helping out with the youth. What can I do?"

Stay as far away from our children as possible. That's what you can do!

Quite frankly, these white folks just really messed up my thing.

Like I said, I ain't a bigot or nothing. They should just go where that kind of stuff is going to be offered.

Then my children started asking all sorts of questions, the most memorable of which was, "Hey dad, what would you think if one of us married one of the white kids? Would you be mad?"

OHMYGOD!

HOLDUP...WAIT A MINUTE...WAIT ONE MINUTE!

That's why I didn't want them anywhere near our children; they had poisoned their minds already. I was shocked and mortified by the very thought.

I'm not against black folks and white folks getting married or nothing, just as long as the black folks ain't my kids!

I ain't a bigot or...

"OF COURSE YOU ARE, HAMAN."

What? Who's voice was that?!!!

"YOU KNOW EXACTLY WHOSE VOICE THIS IS."

God knows me. I'm a Christian pastor, not a bigot. How could God say something like this about me?

Hell-looo, this is Haman you're talking to, God. Haman Cross, Jr. You know, the black Haman Cross, Jr.? You know the black Haman Cross, Jr. who's been praying, talking to, and dealing with white folks my entire—and I mean entire—life; that Haman Cross,

Jr. How could I be a bigot?

"I KNOW EXACTLY WHAT HAMAN I'M SPEAKING TO. YOU ARE A BIGOT, HAMAN. NOW PUT DOWN THE KNIFE!"

This was the beginning of God's conviction of me for using that lie—that I wasn't a bigot—over and over and over again.

God has a way of not letting His people, the people who love Him, off the hook easily. He will keep at us, knocking, sometimes even pounding on the doors of our hearts and minds, not letting us rest until we see things the way He sees them. Where did I get off questioning how the white folks got into my church?

All I had to do was a little deductive reasoning. Now, it was a fact that white folks were in my church. They were there every week smiling and happy—*happy*—to be there. And it looked as though more were coming. Okay, but it's a church—my church that I started—for African Americans, remember?

White folks were coming and joining my church, and there was only two ways that they got there: either God sent them or the devil did.

It didn't take very long for me to figure out that Satan had nothing to do with what was beginning to happen at Rosedale Park Baptist Church (The Ideal African American Church). No longer could I continue to ignore the fact that I was accountable to God. I was slapped in the face with the fact that I was a man of God. I was a Pastor of a church—His Church. His Church is not some exclusionary club. It was just like one of those great vacation packages that we all look for, *all-inclusive*.

All-inclusive: black, white, yellow, red, rich, poor, tall, short, fat, skinny, healthy and sick people who were broken and needed everything from minor repairs to major overhauling. God's church is open to all of us. My goal in life, more than anything else, is to please God, and because this was true, it was time for me to act like it. Prove it. I did not want to stand before God saying, *"Sorry God, but that wasn't part of the program. I wanted to help black folks. I didn't want to accommodate my white brothers and sisters."*

God began to allow me to see and feel what whites must feel like when they minister to other cultures. God let me know that it is hard to have a black church—any church—become cross-cultural. I guess I thought whites should just become cross-cultural for the sake of Christ without realizing how difficult this really is. I can now appreciate some of the changes they had to make to share the gospel, especially with black folks in America.

Just as Jesus sent His disciples out into the world with The Great Commission, to take His Word to the world, we Christians have been charged with the same great commission.

But you will receive power when the Holy Spirit comes on you; and you will be my witnesses in Jerusalem, and in all Judea and Samaria, and to the ends of the earth. - Acts 1:8

We are to take His Word to the people to whom we can easily relate; who are just like us; to the place that we feel most comfortable; into our own cities and homes (Jerusalem). We are also to take His Word to the country that we live in and its people. This is further away but we're still fairly comfortable with it (Judea). Less comfortable, but equally important, we are to take His Word to exotic, faraway places that might not otherwise hear His Word (the ends of the earth).

I had read this verse many times in my life, but now God made it personal. God revealed something very important to me as the pastor of the Ideal African American Church. I think I'm like most Christians today. If I had things my way, this is about as far as I would go with the Great Commission. Had it been up to me, I would have started and developed my inner-city African American Church, and I would have been more than happy!

My church family and I would have taken our message all over Detroit (Jerusalem). When we felt the need, we would go out to other inner-cities and to rural black folk—you know, trips to New York, Chicago, L.A., and a trip or two down south every year (Judea). That would have been cool. And the ends of the earth? Oh yeah, we would take trips to Africa, Asia, Jamaica, and the Bahamas. Yeah, that's what I'm talking about!

But Jesus mentioned another place in that scripture, Samaria.

Samaria is the place where our faith is tested and stretched. This is an important part of this scripture for America, because Jews did not want to have anything to do with Samaritans. The Samaritans were beneath contempt. Jews, during the time of the apostles, thought that the Samaritans were dogs. They didn't want to live near them, or come into contact with them. Jews would rather go anywhere—anywhere at all, than Samaria. The Bible is clear to show that the disciples took great pains—even venturing further on their trips, to go around Samaria. This is a place and a people which, were it left up to us (man), would not receive God's Word from anyone, let alone us! Samaria is a place that we don't want to go.

"HELLO! DOES THIS SOUND FAMILIAR, HAMAN? DID YOU READ THAT PART OF MY WORD?"

I had read it before. I had placed it in my heart, the place that wants to please my Lord more than anything. My flesh had been having big problems with the verse, however.

HELLO! Christians of America, DOES THIS SOUND FAMILIAR?

Samaria.

In the church—in His Church—in America today, we are too comfortable and/or afraid to put our faith in God and break down the wall between Jerusalem and Samaria, rich and poor, country and city, black and white.

This was much tougher than I had ever thought. I hadn't needed to face these issues until white folks began to join my African American middle class church. Just as He did when He dropped the veil in front of Peter, God began to re-create and clarify for me what my vision for the church—God's Church, really should be.

In Acts 10:13-15, God says to Peter, *"Get up, Peter. Kill and eat!" "Surely not, Lord!" Peter replied. "I have never eaten anything profane or unclean." The voice spoke to him a second time," Do not call anything impure that God has made clean."*

Essentially, this is the way the church of America, with all of its bigotry and partiality, has responded to God when confronted with what God wants His Church to be. "Not us, God. We don't worship with the profane, unclean, slanted-eyes, thicker-lipped, straighter-hair, different-colored skinned. Let the profane, the unclean, and the different worship their own God. We choose to worship You."

What kind of real worship is this?

God's message to Peter was not that different from the one He gave me. God gave me a unique opportunity to visualize what a Christian committed to reconciliation should look like. God asked me to put down the knife of bigotry. He moved me toward breaking down walls.

I could probably shock you with stories of partiality among God's people, but prejudice in the church community at large is just a reflection of what is in the heart of individual Christians, just as it was with Peter.

I was not led to write this book to point fingers at everyone else. I've already told you that I held bigoted attitudes. The purpose of this book is to show you how God helped me put off those attitudes. I still have a ways to go, believe me, but God has certainly dealt with me about this issue over the years.

I'm reminded of the time that my dad took me to a carnival. What made this trip special was that my dad allowed me to get into a fight! In one of the booths was a balloon in the shape of a man. My ol' man took me up to that balloon man and said, "Haman, punch that balloon man."

I really liked that, because my dad had never actually given me permission to hit anyone before. I jumped at the chance. I punched that balloon-man right in the face. I hit it really hard and knocked him down.

Yeah that's what happens when Haman Cross, Jr. lays a lick on...

Before I knew it, that thing was right back up in my face, and it bopped me right back with his head! I really punched him the next time, but every time I punched it, it popped back up! I'd hit it with all my might. It'd still come back. It was relentless. It always returned to its original upright position.

"Hit it, Haman. Hit it harder," my Dad said.

I went at it; it still came back up. Then he told me to kick it. I let out a yell that would rival any of those guys in martial arts flicks. "Aiiiahhh!" That balloon popped up faster and with more force than it had on all the previous times I assaulted it.

Finally, my dad asked me, "Why does it keep coming back up when you knock it down?"

I didn't know. I shrugged my shoulders and tried to keep from crying.

"It must have something to do with what's on the inside," my Dad explained.

So it is with us. The government can legislate, regulate and entitle all it wants to. There's no amount of legislation, regulation or entitlement that the government can enact to eliminate partiality. Partiality or prejudice will fall down, but then it will continue to bounce back up. Ultimately the problem is inside of us. We must go to the heart of the issue—our hearts! Inside our hearts there is a wall that we must bust down.

Most of us agree that there must be unity in the Body of Christ if we are to do the work that Christ commissioned us to do. Yet do we really know how far we have to go in our own mind-sets? Do we really know how much God has to do in us individually?

This book is about my journey to God's heart concerning separatism and partiality. It hasn't always been easy.

God showed me what bigotry and partiality looked like—up close and personal—and my love for God forced me to *Cross Colors*!

2

CROSS COLORS

"Each time a man stands up for an ideal, or acts to improve the lot of others, or strikes out against injustice, he sends forth a tiny ripple of hope. And crossing each other from a million different centers of energy and daring, those ripples build a current that can sweep down the mightiest walls of oppression and resistance."
- Robert Kennedy
(Address to the National Union of South African Students, Cape Town, South Africa June 7, 1966)

In the late 1980's, Americans added a new term to our collective vocabulary—The Drive-By Shooting. We read about them every day in the newspapers, and saw the aftermath of them on the evening news. Churches across our country were shown filled with weeping parents. We saw them weeping in pain, over the caskets of another child, our future, who would be buried. Many times these children, the next generation, were innocents who had nothing at all to do with the gang war for which they were now a casualty.

California was especially affected by "the drive-by." It could occur for any number of reasons, but sometimes it was simply because the victim was wearing the wrong color clothing. In certain cities on the West Coast, if you were seen wearing the wrong color or particular combination of colors, you could become a drive by shooting victim. The color in the Crips 'hood might include red bandanas. So if you happened to be in another gang's 'hood with a red bandana on, you might find yourself in serious trouble; literally killed because of a color!

During that time, California-based clothing designers, TJ Walker and Carl Jones, developed the idea of a clothing line—Cross Colours—that would use many different colors that would not communicate prejudice, denote gang insignia, or partiality.

What an interesting way of thinking about race problems in America! It's an even more interesting way to think about how the church of America should be dealing with OUR problem. Black, white, red, yellow and brown. The Church includes all of these colors, but how many American churches include all of these colors? How many American churches actually *Cross Colors*?

This is an example of the world doing something that the Church should not only be mirroring but should be leading. If a clothing line like Cross Colours could see past color lines and promote reconciliation and peace, shouldn't God's people and Church be convicted if we are not leading the way? Especially since we have the Prince of Peace as our Lord and Savior!

I was totally convicted.

As I look back, I'll be the first to admit that it has been difficult to become a Cross Colors church. It was more convenient to be bigoted. It was easier to preach—really get down—when I looked out into an audience of folks who looked, talked, and acted the way I did. Folks who—if I wanted to go there—could go there with me:

Don't white folks get on your last nerve? If they do, shout Amen!
Aay-men!

I was just like Peter, perfectly happy to walk around preaching God's love and the Gospel of Jesus Christ and still not wanting to break bread—communion—with those who were not like me. I loved opening God's Word—just as long as I opened the Word to people like me. I was supported in this idea by Christians—both black and white—who have never crossed colors, and have no intentions of going there.

CROSS COLORS: AMERICAN CHRISTIANITY IN BLACK AND WHITE

It is easier to worship with those who are just like you. It's easy to be a Christian around those who know the same songs, and sing them with the same rhythm as you do. How many times have you heard white folks sing, "I know it was the blood?" And if they did sing it, it wasn't the way we sang it in our church. You don't have to explain things. You don't have to slow down or speed up. You don't have to worry about showing emotion, lifting a hand in praise, or cuttin' a step and dancing for Jesus if you feel like doing it!

These things may appear to be minor, but they are some of the things that prevent us from crossing colors. Just look around—it's not just whites worshipping with whites and blacks worshipping with blacks. Korean, Latinos, Nigerians, and Romanian Christians do the same thing.

The Lord, through His Word, has made it perfectly clear that His Church is to be unified. But collectively, the Church has taken a back seat in the ongoing struggle for racial reconciliation. We all were given the instruction to begin to *Cross Colors*. Unfortunately, we have given Satan ground in this fight. We have fallen into his trap of death.

The Bible tells us that faith without works is dead. So, every January when churches throughout America celebrate Rev. Dr. Martin Luther King, Jr.'s birthday, we try to do a little CPR on the dead body that was once our hope of racial reconciliation. We pinch its nose and give the dead body of Christian love a few deep breaths before we spend the next year forgetting what Dr. King and many others died for in this country. It's futile and superficial for the most part.

Imagine if we literally tried to resuscitate a human body that had been dead for a year. Well, it really is the same. One day of thinking, singing and praying about racial reconciliation does nothing over the long haul.

We have also given our detractors reason to question our Christian philosophy and values, since we ourselves can't seem to agree or get along. The critics of the contemporary Christian church have had success in writing us off as "hysterical radicals," in great part because of the backbiting and infighting among us, in the church at large and between black and white Christians in particular. Not only has this given our detractors reason to question our Christian philosophy, but it has also led many to question Christ Himself.

Forgive us, Lord!

For Christ's love compels us, because we are convinced that one died for all, and therefore all died. And he died for all, that those who live should no longer live for themselves but for him who died for them and was raised again. So from now on we regard no one from a worldly point of view. Though we once regarded Christ in this way, we do so no longer. Therefore, if anyone is in Christ, He is a new creation; the old has gone, the new has come! All this is from God, who reconciled us to himself through Christ and gave us the ministry of reconciliation: that God was reconciling the world to himself in Christ , not counting people's sins against them. And he has committed to us the message of reconciliation. We are therefore Christ's ambassadors, as though God were making his appeal through us. - 2 Corinthians 5:14-20a

Paul calls it the ministry of reconciliation. Some contemporary Christians refer to it as bridging a divide. But I call it "bustin' a wall!" In America, that means "bustin' a wall"—a very large, very thick wall—made up of ignorance, hatred, misunderstanding, fear, arrogance, and quite a few "isms."

I hope that we will all prayerfully consider what lifestyle adjustments and changes God would have us make to hasten this reconciliation without delay. Conviction. Confession. Asking forgiveness. Repentance. Reconciliation. Restitution. That's what God's love and His body is all about: changing us into what He wants us to be, into the kind of Church He wants us to be.

I wanted to please God no matter what. That was my goal. If being a cross-cultural church was what He wanted, that's what I would do. I would welcome all different kinds of folks into my church. I would change my mission statement into His mission statement.

I would *Cross Colors* even if no one else wanted to. I would submit to my Lord. All it would require of me would be to have faith in "bustin' a wall,"—the wall—of bigotry and racism in my own heart. All it would require of me would be to face the lies in my life and expose them to the Light.

All it would require of me was dying to self.

3

Manna: What is It?

> *"We hold these truths to be self-evident, that all men are created equal, that they are endowed by their Creator with certain unalienable Rights, that among these are Life, Liberty and the pursuit of Happiness."*
> *- Thomas Jefferson*
> *("The Declaration of Independence")*

God isn't into partiality. The entire discussion begins and ends right there. Oh how it grieves God's heart and mine that the discussion doesn't end there, however! As I told you earlier, that wasn't always the case with me.

God confronted me about my bigoted mindset. This was to be the first and most important wall that I would have to bust down.

It was easy to see all the prejudice and partiality in the actions, hearts and minds of white America, but I wasn't able to see my own stuff.

The first thing God showed me was that the "Ideal African American Church" that I wanted to create so badly was not my church—it was His. I had my own ideas about what Rosedale Park Baptist Church should look like. But obviously, God had His ideas too. The mere fact that God had brought whites to a church that had no intention of inclusion to begin with should have given me a hint as to whose hand was really involved in forming His Church.

Then it occurred to me: I hadn't done any sermons aimed at bringing in white folks. As a matter of fact, I had been preaching and teaching the Word—I thought—solely with black folks in mind.

When God spoke to me about letting go of the knife of partiality, He began to empower me with the ideas and the tools I needed to do just what He had asked. The first thing He did was to get me to think in a new way, by redefining words and phrases that had become a part of my everyday vocabulary and life.

God spoke to me and said, "HAMAN, YOU MUST TEAR DOWN THE WALL OF PREJUDICE AND PARTIALITY IN YOUR OWN HEART FIRST."

At first this seemed insane. Here I was, a black man; born and raised in America; a descendant of slaves; treated as a second class citizen; a victim of bigotry, inequality and racism my entire life; and I have prejudice and partiality in my heart?

And what was up with this partiality thing? The issue is race, isn't it? Isn't this whole thing rooted in racial divisiveness, and perpetuated by people who preach hate and anger?

I went to the Bible to see what it said about race. If God wanted me to deal with another race, surely there are scriptures that show what He thinks of it.

I looked throughout the Bible searching for the word "race" (and not the one that involves your feet). It wasn't in there—not anywhere. I was shocked at first. I found a concordance and did a study of scriptures that had to do with what I considered racism. It is not in there. I could not believe it!

Any 21st century American could give you a laundry list of all the pain, suffering and death that had stemmed directly from racism. We have an entire vocabulary of words that function as synonyms for racism: Holocaust, ethnic cleansing, genocide, Apartheid, and segregation to name a few. They were not only a part of my vocabulary; they had become a part of my life! Why weren't they addressed in God's Word with the one word that summed them up? It wasn't in there!

How could something so important not be addressed? How could God have forgotten to talk about this? As much as my people and I have been affected by it; as much as it meant to the history of this country; how did Jesus not teach on this issue?

Could it be that this whole race thing wasn't that important to God? No way! I had heard white Christians use that "curse of Ham" thing enough to make me sick. I had heard people try to justify slavery and segregation with the Bible, and I was not going to accept that God had not addressed the biggest issue between black and white Christians. I knew that this whole issue was important, so I dug deeper into the Word. What I found showed me clearly where God's heart is concerning bigotry and racism. God does clearly address prejudice, racism and bigotry. He does not use our 21st Century vocabulary, however.

I discovered that God does speak to us about bigotry, inequality and prejudice in the Church, but He calls it something else—*partiality*.

But his brothers hated Joseph because of their father's partiality. They couldn't say a kind word to him. - Genesis 37:4 (NLT)

To show partiality is not good—yet a person will do wrong for a piece of bread. - Proverbs 28:21

So I have caused you to be despised and humiliated before all the people, because you have not followed my ways but have shown partiality in matters of the law. - Malachi 2:9

Then Peter replied, "I see very clearly that God doesn't show partiality." - Acts 10:34 (NLT)

I tend to think that we have enough words in our vernacular that we don't need to add new ones to say basically what the old ones are already saying. So as God began the work in me to *Cross Colors*, at first I thought, why don't we just call a spade a spade? If somebody is a racist, just call him or her racist. If somebody is a bigot, just call him or her a bigot, right? We don't need another word to add to the vocabulary of racial issues in America, do we?

But I realized that the word *partiality* has probably been around a lot longer, which meant that these words, like "race," had come along later. As I dug deeper, I found that the idea of "races" isn't even something that would have been mentioned within the Bible because our definitions of race and racial differences have come from man, not God.

Our society has come up with all of these opinions and definitions of race, but race isn't even really a physiological issue. It is a sociological issue. We have allowed our sinful nature, which would have us separate from each other and ultimately from God, to overshadow what both science and the Bible teach us about ourselves.

"Some people think that there must be different 'races' of people because there appear to be major differences between various groups, such as skin color and eye shape. The truth, though, is that these so-called 'racial characteristics' are only minor variations among groups of people. Scientists have found that if one were to take any two people from anywhere in the world, the basic genetic differences between these two people would typically be around 0.2 percent—even if they came from the same people group. But, these so-called 'racial' characteristics that many think are major differences (skin color, eye shape, etc.) account for only 6 percent of this 0.2 percent variation, which amounts to a mere 0.012 percent difference genetically. In other words, the so-called 'racial' differences are absolutely trivial (from "One Blood: The Biblical Answer to Racism" by Ken Ham, Carl Wieland and Don Batten)."

Then God said, "Let us make man in our image, in our likeness, and let them rule over the fish of the sea and the birds of the air, over the livestock, over all the earth, and over all the creatures that move along the ground." So God created man in His own image, in the image of God He created him; male and female He created them. - Genesis 1:26-27

God did not create a black Adam, a brown Adam or a white Adam. He created Adam, in His own image, which means that we are relational, that we love and care for each other. If we are going to use the word "race," then in its proper scientific and Biblical context, it pertains to the human race. We are all of the same race, created by a God that loves us all and wants us to love each other and to love Him in return.

Now we can look at racism or partiality for what it really is: a social disease. It is a disease that started outside our bodies and has moved to the inside. Because of its nature, as a social disease, we must wipe it out if we are to ever be healthy.

I looked at the scriptures that talked about partiality again. It was all right there in black and white (pun intended). As God opened it up to me, I realized that I could preach a sermon on each of those scriptures just from my experience alone.

I looked up partiality in the dictionary.

Partiality (pär´-shê-âl´-a-të) adj. 1. Not total; incomplete. 2. Biased; prejudiced (The American Heritage Dictionary).

There it was – in black and white. **Not total. Incomplete. Biased. Prejudiced**. It was everything you always wanted to know about racism but were afraid to ask. Hadn't I felt like an unwelcomed alien in a foreign land many times when I attended white churches? I've since talked to many whites who can identify with that feeling when they have visited black churches (lest we forget that partiality is an equal opportunity sin). How many times in my life had I sat in "fellowship" with the "saints" and felt: "not total; incomplete?"

I paid careful attention to the scripture from Acts once again. Church of America, no matter what we would like to think, we must realize that when God began growing the Church, He had to break down the walls of partiality in the heart of the disciple Peter, the rock on which He built the Church! The reason He did this is because He did not want it infecting His Church! He didn't like it then and He doesn't like it now!

Then Peter replied, "I see very clearly that God doesn't show partiality." - Acts 10:34 (NLT)

Partiality is at work in all of our lives. Whether you are in the majority or the minority, your life and the lives of your family are affected by it. It is sin. It is dangerous and antithetical to God's Church. It has been chewing away at the fabric of this country forever, and if it is not confronted and destroyed, it will destroy our families, our churches, our nation and ultimately injure the Church—God's Church. Look at the first instance in Scripture where the word appears to see what it does within a family, a picture of the community of faith.

But his brothers hated Joseph because of their father's partiality. They couldn't say a kind word to him. - Genesis 37:4 (NLT)

This is *America*.

Black, white, brown, red, and yellow Christians hate each other because of partiality, and we cannot say a kind word to each other. As Christians we are sadly, "not total; incomplete."

Do not for a second entertain the idea that I am comparing God to Jacob. Our Heavenly Father is not Jacob. He does not show partiality. Even though our Father does not show partiality, we still have a tendency to act like the children of Jacob rather than the children of Light.

What's up with that?

Oh, we talk about loving each other, but do we really? If we really loved each other, would 11 a.m. Sunday morning still be the most segregated hour of the week?

I looked at all of this, thought about what part in this I had played and I was filled with shame. It totally grieved my heart. I thought about what a shameful witness I was. Then another thought occurred to me: If I was feeling like that, what was God feeling and thinking of us?

Meditate on that for a moment.

The chief food substance of the Israelites during their forty years in the wilderness was "bread from heaven." Upon seeing it on the ground every morning, the Israelites said, *"Manna."* This means "What is it?" What "it" was, was a replacement for food; a replacement that God provided for them — bread from heaven.

In today's lexicon we call the actual bread of heaven "manna," and we consider manna a noun. The Hebrews used it as a query—"What is it?" When I thought of what God must think of partiality among His people, it made me wonder if He was saying the same thing about what we call serving Him through our love for each other. "MANNA— WHAT IS IT?"

Unlike the manna that God sent the children of Israel however, what we are calling Christian love and worship and presenting to Him is falling far short of the mark. When Christ was asked what the greatest commandment was, he replied:

Love the Lord your God with all your heart and with all your soul and with all your mind. This is the first and greatest commandment. And the second is like it: Love your neighbor as yourself. All the Law and the Prophets hang on these two commandments. - Matthew 22:37-40

When we look at our country and its divide, can we truly say that we have ever even seen this verse? Can Christians in America be proud of what we have allowed our church and ultimately our country to become? I thought I was doing exactly what God wanted me to do; starting the Ideal African American church. Yet I was so far off the mark, I couldn't even see the target. I was happy and secure in my piousness and righteousness.

...all our righteous acts are like filthy rags... - Isaiah 64:6a

If even our righteousness is like filthy rags to God, what a stench this so-called Christian church of America must be in His nostrils! My own sin was enough to make me sick. What was it doing to God?

And do not grieve the Holy Spirit of God, with whom you were sealed for the day of redemption. - Ephesians 4:30

Look a little further into Genesis at how Jacob reacted when he was shown Joseph's coat.

Then Jacob tore his clothes, put on sackcloth and mourned for his son many days. All his sons and daughters came to comfort him, but he refused to be comforted. "No," he said, "I will continue to mourn until I join my son in the grave." So his father wept for him. - Genesis 37:34-35

This is not to suggest that God shows partiality, as Jacob did. However, I can imagine that He certainly is grieved by how His children treat each other. And if this supposition is true, we, the same people who commit the injury every day, will not be able to comfort Him, just as Jacob's sons could not comfort Jacob. Are we going to be like the Israelites to whom God was speaking in Malachi?

"A son honors his father, the servant his master. If I am a father, where is the honor due me? If I am a master, where is the respect due me?" says the Lord Almighty. "It is you, O priests, who show contempt for my name. But you ask, 'How have we shown contempt for your name?' You place defiled food on my altar. But you ask, 'How have we defiled you?' By saying that the Lord's table is contemptible. When you bring blind animals for sacrifice, is that not wrong? When you sacrifice crippled or diseased animals, is that not wrong? Try offering them to your governor! Would he be pleased with you? Would he accept you?" says the Lord Almighty. - Malachi 1:6-8

I'm sure God is saying, "MANNA—WHAT IS IT?" about this whole partiality thing. God will not and does not accept our playing church. We show contempt for our Lord when we play at our love for each other and worship of Him. He is not going to accept our—lets watch for this word in our vocabularies—"tolerance" of each other while we sit together at ecumenical events, and while we join arms on Rev. Dr. Martin Luther King, Jr's birthday remembrances.

It does nothing for God when we sing songs and cry and pray together at Promise Keepers meetings, and then run back to our churches— black, white, yellow or whatever—and do nothing until we have to do it again the next year.

How many lay members, deacons, pastors, and entire churches worship every Sunday morning knowing that no one of a different race is going to visit, let alone join their church, and want to keep it that way?

It is you, O priests, who show contempt for my name.

So, let's admit that the way we treat each other grieves God and shows the world that when we act this way toward each other as Christians, we are the hypocrites that they all think we are. We will not only have a poor witness as long as we resist crossing colors, but we will continue to show contempt for our God, all of which grieves Him deeply. Let's also admit that this is a sin and that we must fight it in order to defeat it.

Don't make the mistake of calling it anything other than a sin, because it is a sin. If we approach this as just a "problem" or a "misunderstanding," we will not pray like we should, and we will not fight like we should. This is just what Satan wants us to do. If we treat it for what it is, then we will defeat it. But if we continue to take the issue of partiality lightly, we allow Satan to gain more of a foothold in our lives, our churches and in the lives of the people whom we are supposed to evangelize.

We must confess our sin and begin to repent. I can't confess your sin for you. I can only confess mine and ask for forgiveness. I can, however, give you some ideas of how you go about repenting—turning away from — that sin.

I don't want to sugar-coat this: this is going to take some work. All repentance takes work. It may take a lot of work for some and less work for others. It requires that we face some tough issues, but never forget that God is there to give us the grace to conquer the problem.

This is what I faced.

I had dealt with whites just as many black men in America deal with whites—only when it benefited me, or when I absolutely had to. Beyond those two scenarios, I felt that seeing a white person was not going to make or break my day. An eye for an eye, and tooth for a tooth was a scripture that was tattooed on my forehead, especially when it came to dealing with white folks! I was good at it too. If a white cop rousted me or anybody else I knew, I took he next opportunity to dump on a white person. When I saw or even perceived some racism in the church, I acted a stone fool: insulting white Christians, threatening, doing my best to let them know that I SEE YOU—*youphonythinlippednocolorhonky.*

When I was a kid, there were many little white boys at Christian summer camps and fellowships that caught a beat down from Haman Cross, Jr., THE NEGRO AVENGER. In my mind that's what black power meant—beating down somebody white! *Come over here, white boy, and let me show you some real black power— BAM, BAM!* As far as I could see, black power never, ever was about the uplifting and empowering of black people and culture, but the absolute hatred of and retaliation against white people.

I was saved from that attitude so long ago that it is actually painful to recall some of those memories. I didn't realize or care at the time that my actions were wounding not only the people of God but God as well. When God began to convict me of my own sin, I saw how much I had let the devil use me. I cried when I realized that in my pain and anger, I helped many white Christians either begin to erect their own walls of prejudice and separation, or added brick and mortar to the one that they had going already. I had no idea that just because of my walls, and not dealing with them, that I was affecting so many people so negatively. When we do not accept the challenge to bring about reconciliation, we say NO to Christ's desire that the church be one: united.

My prayer is not for them alone. I pray also for those who will believe in me through their message, that all of them may be one, Father, just as you are in me and I am in you. May they also be in us so that the world may believe that you have sent me. I have given them the glory that you gave me, that they may be one as we are one: I in them and you in me. May they be brought to complete unity to let the world know that you sent me and have loved them even as you have loved me. - John 17:20-23

As Christians living in America, we, the Church, must unite to face the incredible challenges that confront our society. The Bible is full of examples of people coming together to win victories for our Lord. For instance, the apostles, with their diverse backgrounds, came together to "upset the world" with the message of the Gospel. In addition, David's mighty men united with the common goal of making David king.

When you read the list of the men who fought for David during his military campaigns, pay attention to the diversity among the ranks. Ammonites, Ahohites, Hararites, Harodites, Netophathites and others were all involved in and part of God's plan.

I recently traveled to Israel with a group of American pastors. We met and prayed with Jewish, Ethiopian and Gentile pastors. When I looked out over the large gathering and saw the great diversity of the men gathered, it reminded me that this is what pleases God — the whole of His creation at work to do His will.

The differences of the apostles were lost once they allowed the Holy Spirit to use them the way He wanted to use them. Think of the world now. Even though there are yet many unbelievers, the name of Jesus is widely known even among the unsaved. It wasn't like this in the first-century church. Twelve apostles began something that has toppled cities, governments and empires over the course of human history.

They all joined together constantly in prayer, along with the women and Mary the mother of Jesus, and with his brothers. In those days Peter stood up among the believers (a group numbering about a hundred and twenty) Those who accepted his message were baptized, and about three thousand were added to their number that day. They devoted themselves to the apostles' teaching and to fellowship, to the breaking of bread and to prayer. Everyone was filled with awe at the many wonders and signs performed by the apostles. All the believers were together and had everything in common. - Acts 1:14-15, 2:41-44

The Book of Acts tells us that the first Church had 120 members — men and women with different backgrounds — yet they had all things in common and they added to their number daily. This is the model of the Church that we must identify with. After receiving the Holy Spirit, the apostles were able to speak the languages of many different people, so that they could communicate and spread the Gospel to them. They had new minds.

In confronting me with my own bigotry, God helped me realize that white American Christians, African American Christians — all American Christians — need to learn new and different ways of communicating, as well as receive a new mindset.

We need to change our adjectives when we talk to or about each other. Instead of being African American Christians or Mexican American Christians, we need to be Christians who happen to be white Americans, or Christians who just happen to be Mexican and so on.

I don't say this lightly. The more adjectives that we use to precede "Christian" not only moves us further and further away from Christ (both literally and figuratively), but also moves us closer to apostasy.

Hi. I'm Haman Cross, Jr. and I'm a *middleagedafricanamericanmaleslayedinthespiritbiblebelievingbaptizedintheholyspirit* Christian.

I am all of those things. But my first commitment—my first love—must be to Christ. Correcting our syntax might seem minor or insignificant, but remember, it's the little things that often trip us up. Referring to myself as an African American Christian puts my ethnicity and culture ahead of my Lord. My race, which includes who I am to America, becomes not only how I define myself, but also how I am defined. This is the attitude that is prevalent in America, and this is one of the many small things that make up one huge thing that keeps us separate and divided.

I asked this question of myself and it is a question that we all must ponder. What's more important: our ethnicity or our Christianity? By considering myself and calling myself an African-American Christian, would it be more important to me to fight for African American issues and causes or for Christian issues and causes? The lines become blurred and before we know it, you have so-called Christians screaming in each other's faces and showing the world just what being a Christian means to us—absolutely nothing good.

Hi I'm_____. I'm an African American Christian.

As I look at the statement now with "new" eyes, it makes me wonder if the African American Christian has an agenda that has nothing to do with Christ. If this seems like that to me, what must it sound like to other non-African American Christians?

What if someone walked up to you and introduced themselves as a pro-choice Christian, a right-to-life Christian or a gay rights Christian? Do you see where I'm going?

I got to thinking about how this must sound to other non-black Christians, then wondered what God must think?

I don't know about anyone else, but when I come before my Lord, I don't want Him to say to me: "HEY HAMAN, YOU'RE THE AFRICAN AMERICAN CHRISTIAN RIGHT? WELL, I WANT

YOU TO GO BACK DOWN THERE AND ASK ALL THE AFRICAN AMERICANS TO LET YOU INTO THEIR HOUSES, BECAUSE I DON'T HAVE A SPOT FOR YOU UP HERE!"

I do not want to hear that, just because I thought who I am is more important than Whose I am.

No, what I want to hear is "WELL DONE MY GOOD AND FAITHFUL SERVANT!"

We must unite to fight our common enemies—the devil, the world, our flesh, secularism, humanism, racism and the millions of other "isms" that are out here to destroy us.

We must affirm each other despite our cultural and racial distinctiveness. When each of us became a Christian, we were called to a new cultural loyalty. Our identity changed, and our allegiance became singular. We must be true to Jesus Christ!

Even us, whom he also called, not only from the Jews but also from the Gentiles? As he says in Hosea: "I will call them 'my people' who are not my people; and I will call her 'my loved one' who is not my loved one," and, "In the very place where it was said to them, 'You are not my people,' there they will be called 'children of the living God.'" - Romans 9:24-26

Let's for a moment really look at partiality—what it really is. No matter what you want to call it—prejudice, bigotry, racism—it's wrong and dangerous. It hinders communication among the people of God. In doing this, it enhances Satan's communication with us instead of God's. When we practice and encourage partiality, we are continuing to give ground to Satan in our Christian lives. By trying to ignore it because it's a painful or volatile subject, we don't move forward. If we are not moving forward, we are still relinquishing ground to Satan. We cannot continue this way, with our communication shut down and our bodies sitting still. We cannot fulfill the commission that Christ entrusted to us.

The reason God had to show Peter the vision about his bigotry was so that the Gospel could be spread.

And I tell you that you are Peter, and on this rock I will build my church, and the gates of Hades will not overcome it. - Matthew 16:18

And keep this in mind. In order to get Peter to understand and begin to do something about his own partiality, God had to put Peter in a trance! Do we think that crying about our partiality and asking for forgiveness is all that it is going to take to heal us? Should we think this? NO! It is going to take some work. And we must— MUST—do this if we are going to spread the Good News of Jesus Christ.

That snapshot from the growth of the Church is included in Scripture to teach us about how deep, and how strong partiality is ingrained within us. It's also there to confront us about how we intend to deal with partiality in our own lives. Peter was not going to be able to effectively share the Gospel—to the ends of the earth— if he didn't learn that lesson. Trust me, no matter how many Gentiles would have heard the Good News of Jesus Christ from Peter, if he had treated them as unclean, he was going to be a stumbling block for them in receiving the Gospel.

When any Israelite or any alien living in Israel separates himself from me and sets up idols in his heart and puts a wicked stumbling block before his face and then goes to a prophet to inquire of me, I the LORD will answer him myself. I will set my face against that man and make him an example and a byword. I will cut him off from my people. Then you will know that I am the LORD. - Ezekiel 14:7-8

Peter took him aside and began to rebuke him. "Never, Lord!" he said. "This shall never happen to you!" Jesus turned and said to Peter, "Get behind me, Satan! You are a stumbling block to me; you do not have in mind the things of God, but the things of men. Then Jesus said to his disciples, "If anyone would come after me, he must deny himself and take up his cross and follow me. For whoever wants to save his life will lose it, but whoever loses his life for me will find it. - Matthew 16:22-25

Therefore let us stop passing judgment on one another. Instead, make up your mind not to put any stumbling block or obstacle in your brother's way. - Romans 14:13

We put no stumbling block in anyone's path, so that our ministry will not be discredited. - 2 Corinthians 6:3

Partiality is real. It is serious and it is painful. Partiality is antithetical to the Gospel of Jesus Christ. It works to keep us in the dark and blinded to the greater progress we can make as Christians.

The eye is the lamp of the body. If your eyes are good, your whole body will be full of light. But if your eyes are bad, your whole body will be full of darkness. If then the light within you is darkness, how great is that darkness! - Matthew 6:22-23

Just like Peter, we must begin to see things with different eyes. When Peter looked at the food as unclean, he was seeing it through the eyes that he had grown up with. He was seeing the food through the eyes the culture of the times, the culture of his ethnic group, the history of his culture, and even the way his family wanted him to see it. He was seeing with the vision of a people and a culture that had seen miracles accomplished throughout their history, yet could not recognize God when He walked among them. Peter was seeing through sin-covered eyes, the eyes of hypocrites who went through all of the ritual of showing their respect and love for God, but when they had the opportunity to really worship Him, rejected and crucified Him!

All the people answered, "Let his blood be on us and on our children!" - Matthew 27:25

Look at what sin had done in the lives of the Jews of Jerusalem. Their sin was so completely overwhelming that they even cursed their own children! This is a significant point because of the fact that America has brought and continues to bring a curse upon its children by teaching and encouraging them to look at the world through the sinful eyes of partiality. Think of this scripture the next time you tell your children not to play with those kids, or you laugh at a joke that degrades or disrespects an entire race of people!

Sociologists and psychologists across this country agree that we tend to teach our children bigotry. We are responsible for the future and we cannot take this lightly.

He said to them: "You are well aware that it is against our law for a Jew to associate with a Gentile or visit him. But God has shown me that I should not call any man impure or unclean. - Acts 10:28

When Peter saw that he should call nothing unclean that God has made, he was seeing from God's perspective. These were new eyes—eyes that had been given to him because of the death, burial and resurrection of our Lord and Savior Jesus Christ. These are the eyes that we must use as we begin to bust the walls.

The vision didn't change for Peter: God showed it to him three times. Peter had to begin to see things the way that God wanted him to see things. When we do this, we can all look at the same thing and see what God wants us to see, not what our culture, ethnic background, or even our families want us to see.

This inability to see things from God's perspective is why we

CROSS COLORS: AMERICAN CHRISTIANITY IN BLACK AND WHITE

Americans can look at the O.J. Simpson trial, or the fatal shootings of Travyon Martin or Mike Brown and never fully want to, or try to understand why blacks and whites reacted the way they did. Our inability to openly, patiently, and honestly discuss our issues with each other is why we once again hide the whole issue as something that we can't discuss with "them."

Because we have never really tried to understand why blacks feel this way about this issue, or why whites feel that way about that issue, we continue to let the wall between us stand and gain strength. It's always been easier to make assumptions, or decide that communicating might cause more harm than good. If we are to live as Christ did, we must come to grips with the fact that His ministry was all about upsetting the status quo of His day.

If we never learn why we think this way or that way, we will never really care for one another. We will never understand when and why we have wounded and hurt someone, and that is why we are in the predicament we are in today.

Open, honest and patient communication is something that must occur if we are going to *Cross Colors*.

4

❖

Walls (Brick and Mortar)

*"We wear our fingers rough with handling them.
Oh, just another kind of outdoor game,
One on a side. It comes to little more:
There where it is we do not need the wall:
He is all pine and I am apple orchard.
My apple trees will never get across
And eat the cones under his pines, I tell him.
He only says, 'Good fences make good neighbors.'"
- Robert Frost
("Mending Wall")*

The hermit crab spends 90% of its life in a shell. As an infant, it must find a shell to protect it from predators, sickness and nature. It must continue to change shells throughout its life if it is to survive. As it outgrows one shell, it must find another larger shell that will function as its home and protection. To change shells, the crab must find a suitable new shell and crawl into it. At some point, the crab finds itself between shells.

The hermit crab is vulnerable at this point. Shedding one shell for another is intimidating and frightening. The crab has come to depend on its current shell for protection and comfort, and has no clue as to what is awaiting its fragile body during its transition. This is a huge decision, yet one that it must make if it is to survive. If the crab decides not to change its shell, then its current shell will become its coffin. This is nature—part of God's design for the hermit crab. The theory of natural selection tells us that the crabs that make the decision to not change shells shouldn't and won't be allowed to live, thereby keeping the gene pool for the hermit crabs strong, useful and vibrant. It's just the nature of the beast that some of them will not survive.

No big deal—unless you happen to be a hermit crab.

We should all be able to relate to the hermit crab. "I like my group, clique, neighborhood, or Church," we defiantly say. "No matter what you say, I am not changing shells." Ultimately, this attitude will doom us, just like the hermit crab that doesn't want to change shells.

I can understand why the hermit crab is intimidated—I feel you my brother!

To be in-between shells is very dangerous. The hermit crab realizes that if he is in-between shells, the sea current can take him anywhere. Without that protective covering, the hermit crab has no anchor. Without that shell, other sea creatures can devour him.

Likewise, when we begin to consider the prospect of tearing down walls of misconceptions, preconceived ideas and mistrust—walls that have been very strategically placed and erected for generations (remember this)—it's pretty scary. It can be overwhelming. After all, we are tearing down walls that were built and have continued to be fortified for a reason. If we tear down walls and begin to actually become acquainted and in relationship with different people from various cultures and ethnicities, the wall is down—we cannot go back. It can be frightening. If we take the initiative, it makes us very vulnerable. We place ourselves at risk of rejection and pain.

I was scared. Just like the hermit crab, I was frightened. I understood the fear. The objections to tearing down walls are all very familiar to me.

But why are we all so frightened?

Why was I so frightened?

I had been wounded. I had been hurt. It was that simple. This Cross Colors thing that God was confronting me with wasn't something that I was jumping at the chance to get involved in. I wasn't in a hurry to run the risk of being hurt again.

I didn't have to look far for reasons and rationalizations to justify my fears, resistance, and objections either.

The devil and our flesh conspire constantly to get us to open a book that they always have prepared for us to read. We've all read this book before—the huge dog-eared volume of "The Book of Excuses." Depending on the issue, many Christians crack the pages of this book open quicker that they do the Holy Bible! Unlike the scriptures of the Holy Bible though, you don't have to be that well-versed in this book. We can all recite these sayings chapter and verse without any help from a pastor or a concordance.

You know the volume, it has scriptures like these included between its covers:

The gospel according to *Ronnie 7:44—"My parents never attempted this, nor my grandparents before them. Why should I be any different?"*

Patrick 1:23—"I can't try new things."

Bigotry 2:1—"I don't want to know them."

Bigotry 5:76—"They'll just take advantage of me."

Patrick 28: 125—"They probably don't really want to know me."

Songs of Stupidity 8:10—"They hate me, so I hate them right back."

When was the last time you quoted something from this book? As I have walked this long, winding road with God, I have come to absolutely hate this book, but it wasn't always like that. There was a time when I opened this book regularly. As we grow in Christ, we must learn to put our book of idiotic and faithless excuses where it belongs—IN THE GARBAGE.

The only sure way to put it in the garbage is to broaden and deepen our relationship with God the Father, God the Son, and God the Holy Ghost. That is the only way! Accept no substitutes, because they just are not going to work. Those sayings, thoughts or whatever you want to call them, are lies, nothing less! You'll notice that I didn't say that they aren't anything more, because they certainly are. Lies start their treacherous life as just lies, but they soon grow into other more dangerous things. You know the little white lies that we joke about as not hurting anyone? That's a LIE!

If you make my word your home you will indeed be my disciples, you will learn the truth and the truth shall make you free. - John 8:31a-32 (NJB)

Christ spoke of the truth setting you free because He knew that lies bind, entrap, enslave, and will ultimately kill you—not someone else, but YOU.

The thief comes only to steal and kill and destroy. I have come so that they may have life and have it to the full. - John 10:10

How many times do we have to read John 10:10 before we realize that this scripture is just as true as all the rest of the Bible?

This is why it is so important to start right now (even as you read this sentence!) to destroy the lies of man and the devil. And the only way to defeat a lie is with the truth.

I know, I know. It's much easier said than done, especially when we see that these lies have been around for so long that they now appear to be facts. It's hard to break down lies when they have been bred and multiplied by people who many times are just like us—and even people that we love. Sometimes the lies are kept going by the man in the mirror every morning! That's the insidious nature of lies—we even tell them to ourselves about ourselves when we know that they are not the truth. It's difficult, it's painful, but we have to start somewhere.

I had to start somewhere. So I began to understand what the mortar and bricks of these walls surrounding my heart were made of: excuses, fear and lies. The first thing I did was promise myself that I would keep excuses out of everything that I possibly could

That was going to take a lot.

The second thing I promised myself was that I would work to stop fearing the unknown.

That was going to take even more.

The third thing I promised myself was that I would stop believing the lies. That was the big one.

I had to fight to hold onto the truth—the truth of God's Word. I held on with all my might and trusted that with God, all things are possible. This was for real.

To defeat fear and bust down that wall in my life was going to take a huge wrecking ball. I had to bust down this huge wall just so I could begin to see all the other walls in my life.

What was my first excuse?

I did not want to lose my identity as I was bustin' down the wall.

Our identity is something that we have worked most of our lives cultivating and protecting. Our identity is something that we hold onto tooth and nail.

This is me, and they are going to have to accept me the way I am.

That's not who I am.

Lord, You can ask me to work with them, but please, don't ask me to love them.

I grew up on the East Side of Detroit. For those of you who don't know Detroit, that's "Da Hood!" We were all about being hard and tough. Preacher's son or not, I was hard. Admitting that I might actually be scared of something was just was not going to happen. In "Da Hoods" and times that I grew up in, the last thing you wanted was to be scared of something. You didn't want to be known as a punk.

Haman Cross, Jr. might be a lot of things, but I ain't no Punkenstein!

I had spent a lot of time cultivating a certain persona over the course of my life. That's why I was able to do the things that I had done. Being known as a punk or sellout was not going to put any more folks in the pews on Sunday. In fact, it would probably work in reverse. That's what my identity said to me. I knew who I was and what I was about, and opening myself up to white folks was just not something that I was comfortable with doing. I was pretty happy with the person that I had made of Haman Cross, Jr. I had some problems (more than I wanted to admit), but I didn't want to change who I was. I wanted to let people know in no uncertain terms that I wasn't scared. I was hard!

I ain't no PUNK!

I thought of how unfair it was to change, to accommodate, to adjust. I began to believe that adjusting and accommodating could lead to assimilating. I did not want to assimilate. That idea had become a four-letter word in the African American community. Inside the African American community, you don't assimilate into another culture or lifestyle; you just become a sell-out or an Uncle Tom.

Neither of these titles sat well with me.

Haman Cross, Jr., Pastor of Rosedale Park Baptist Church, wasn't Tommin' or selling out for anybody.

I wasn't going there no matter what. That wasn't me.

That is one of the big dangers in tearing down a wall: the people with whom you were once enclosed inside the wall may turn on you.

This is what I was faced with—either being thought of as a Punkenstein, or an Uncle Clarence Thomas!

Yet bustin' this wall meant that I had to admit that I needed help in this matter.

I had to admit that there was a part of me, no matter how big or how small, that feared white people, and in ghetto-speak this meant that I was a punk.

In the hood if you were scared of something, you couldn't just admit it. You did anything and everything you could to prove to people that you weren't scared of it.

You talked about it, I mean dogged it: *I ain't scared of them!*

You confronted it in anger: *If a whitey come walkin' through here, they gonna' get busted up!*

You treated it like it was nothing: *I ain't even thinkin' 'bout a honkey!*

This way no one would ever really know that this thing ever intimidated you. It didn't make any difference if the intimidation was because of fear, a lack of understanding, or just plain ambivalence.

Yet bustin' this wall meant that the fruit of my growth would have me relating to whites, having more whites in my—sorry—God's Church. It meant that some people would say I was assimilating, that I was a sell-out, or an Uncle Tom.

Who was I serving? Who was my Lord? Who did I want to please more, people or God?

I began to see through the curtain of lies. I realized that this thing that I called my identity wasn't anything other than a group of differing walls that I had set up in my life for protection—out of fear. This identity was something that I was using as a shell and was keeping me from bustin' a wall in my life. This was significant because I was really beginning to see the nature of walls in my life—in all people's lives—and it would take the understanding of these walls to bust them down.

We are sometimes reluctant to trust those who are different because we have experienced disappointment with those closest to us. Since that is true, we figure it will be even more painful with those who are different. That's why we fear.

God doesn't give us a task, however, without providing the grace and tools needed to accomplish it. I had the Bible and plenty of experiences in my life that allowed me to see God work. I had seen God deliver people from drug habits. I had seen him raise people up out of comas. Yet, here I was not trusting that He could deliver me from my sin of prejudice! What was up with THAT?

For God hath not given us a spirit of fear; but of power, and of love, and of a sound mind. - 2 Timothy 1:7 (KJV)

I held onto this scripture when God began speaking to me about the wall in my heart. I had to. I trusted God more than anyone else. God had shown me in the past that He would not give me something to do and then withhold the grace and power to do it. I just had to have the faith. I knew that what God was moving me to do was going to take the power of the Holy Spirit to accomplish. After all, I was about to embark on the deepest, darkest journey of wall bustin' that I had ever undertaken in my life.

For me to really take the Gospel of Jesus Christ and bust a wall between blacks and whites in my life would prove to be a huge task. Preparing my heart and mind for the war was going to take a lot. This is most difficult in part because, when you start bustin' a wall, you find that there are so many other walls as well.

As God showed me that I had built a wall against whites, he also showed me that it wasn't the only wall I had built.

I was concentrating on racial walls among the people of God, yet it's important to note that we have a wealth of knowledge on building all sorts of walls in our lives.

Looking back at it, I realized that I just didn't have this one wall in my life. I was a regular brick mason when it came to building walls.

I had a wall against authority, a wall against white people, a wall against women, a wall against this, a wall against that, a wall... a wall... a wall...

Ultimately all these walls added up to a wall that was against God!

That realization scared me senseless! I was blocking God from myself in so many different ways, and blocking Him from moving

through different people on my behalf.
That was even more frightening!
One of my members related a story to me about this once:

"There was a time when God used a relationship with another church member to really bless me. It made me understand more fully how members of the Body of Christ spur each other on to spiritual growth. There was a lot of joy in the fellowship. As a result, I found myself being more open to good close Christian relationships, something that I had been hesitant about because of past disappointments and loss. God used this time with this precious Christian to melt away many of the walls of resistance I had allowed to accumulate around my life. I was so grateful and thankful for that friend.

That friend ended up going home to be with the Lord. I made up in my mind that I would not fall back into old habits. Being newly open to closer relationships, a relationship with a friend of the friend who died began to bud. I distinctly remember having to struggle with the question 'Did I really want friendships?' I had just experienced a loss of another friendship. I didn't like the pain that seems to come with relationships. I decided to relax and let God bless me the way he wanted to bless me, even if I wasn't sure about where the relationship would go. I even remember writing a poem during that time:

> I looked around and the walls were down.
> I really couldn't believe that could happen to me.
> Then I realized that God had used my friend
> To successfully knock them to the ground.
> But now she was gone from my life
> And someone else is trying to get in.
> Quick, call the masons!
> We'll just have to put those walls back up again.
> I went to the phone to dial the number.
> Didn't have to even look it up!
> It was one I knew too well.
> With my hands ready to dial, the Lord began to speak.
> He told me if I called the mason again
> My spiritual growth would be stunted.

I had to accept the pain with the joy.
That was just the way He designed it to be."

From this saint's experience, we can see that building a wall was totally under their control. This helped me to understand that while the bricks and mortar are there at our disposal, the inclination is there also. But no matter what, God gives us a choice to build the wall or not to build it; to keep it up or tear it down.

God was giving me understanding about the nature and make-up of the walls in my life, just as He will give you. We must look at ourselves first, and the walls that we have built in our lives. We must look at what the walls are made of, and then God will begin to equip us with the proper tools to tear it down.

A demolition worker who is given the task of bustin' a wall made of steel, and who walks up to it with a hammer and chisel is:

A. Going to wear himself out because he doesn't have the right tools for the job.

B. Going to injure himself.

C. Going to look like a fool.

D. NOT GOING TO SUCCEED IN HIS ASSIGNMENT!

Before we can begin to do the work to bust a wall, we must understand just what kind of wall we are working on. We must look to God to give us the answer and to show us where we are to start. He will give us all we need to bust any wall.

The Lord tears down the proud man's house... - Proverbs 15:25a

"Is not my word like fire," declares the Lord, "and like a hammer that breaks a rock in pieces?" - Jeremiah 23:29

All Scripture is God-breathed and is useful for teaching, rebuking, correcting and training in righteousness, so that the man of God may be thoroughly equipped for every good work. - 2 Timothy 3:16-17

I had been given the knowledge and the right tools for the job.
Now it was time to get busy—time to start bustin' a wall.

5

❖

Walls (Revisited)

> *"Joshua fit de battle of Jericho an' de walls came tumblin' down…"*
> **Traditional Negro Spiritual**

As I began to look into the walls that I had constructed in my own life, I found myself having to acknowledge not only the destructive nature of walls, but also the importance and positive purposes of walls.

In the Old Testament, there were two cities that had walls surrounding them that were brought to my mind: one in the book of Joshua and the other in the book of Nehemiah.

Before the Children of Israel could get to the Promised Land, they had to go through Jericho. The People of God had to bust down some walls! It was as simple as that.

Jericho was a walled city, which seemed impenetrable. Jericho had strong, fortified walls that were built to keep things and people out. Fortified means to add strength to something. The people of Jericho tended the walls of their city and trusted them to protect them.

HAMAN CROSS, JR.

When they discovered that the people of God were on their way toward Jericho to do some wall bustin', the city closed off all the entrances and exits.

The Bible tells us:

Now the gates of Jericho were securely barred because of the Israelites. No one went out and no one came in. - Joshua 6:1

Now, we can assume that the people of Jericho had some confidence in their city's walls. They were confident because they had helped to fortify the walls themselves. If they had any idea that the walls would not protect them, they would have fled instead of shutting the town up tight. That seems logical doesn't it? Yet, all of this apparent confidence was doing nothing other than covering up fear; plain ordinary fear; just like the hermit crab that does not want to change shells; just like Christians who do not want to *Cross Colors*.

Their confidence was in mortar and brick, and in their hearts they knew that there would be no way that this would stop God from doing what He wanted and fulfilling His promise to the Hebrews.

The fear had them gripped so tightly that for six days they did nothing but watch and listen while Joshua and the children of Israel marched around their city. They didn't even throw a rock at them!

This is just what we do when we decide to tightly shut up our churches, our neighborhoods, and ultimately our hearts in an attempt to make sure that, "No one came out and no one came in."

The people of Jericho were scared because they had heard of the power of God. They knew that when the One True God, the God of Abraham, showed up, walls were going to be busted. Notice what the scripture tells us that Rahab said to the spies of the children of Israel.

...and said to them, "I know that the Lord has given this land to you and that a great fear of you has fallen on us, so that all who live in this country are melting in fear because of you. We have heard how the Lord dried up the water of the Red Sea for you when you came out of Egypt, and what you did to Sihon and Og, the two kings of the Amorites east of the Jordan, whom you completely destroyed. When we heard of it, our hearts melted and everyone's courage failed because of you, for the Lord your God is God in heaven above and on the earth below." - Joshua 2:9-11

Look at the image. Here is a walled city that had protected itself for some time, yet the power of God had preceded Joshua and the Hebrews. The people were doing what they had always done. They were operating out of fear. These were the people of Jericho, who had lived "protected" behind their walls for years. They now believed that God and His people were on the way, and meant to bust a wall—their wall. The king and the people of Jericho knew God was in the mix, and they were doing their best to keep the people of God from bustin' down their walls. It was fear that had them build the walls in the first place, and now it was fear that had them shut up the city so tight that no one came out and no one came in. Look at Joshua 6:1 again.

The city of Jericho was tightly shut up. No one came out and no one came in.

Their fear forced them into a situation that promised that they would be destroyed, for "no one came out and no one came in."

Bigotry depends on not allowing people in or out. Without closed walls, doors, minds and hearts, bigotry and fear can't survive. Bigotry and fear are two things that the enemy depends on to destroy and separate us.

Just as the walls of Jericho came down, so too did the walls of Haman Cross, Jr. I trusted in God to do exactly for me what He did for Joshua and the children of Israel, bust a wall. The walls that we have built are just like the walls of Jericho. These walls make it difficult, if not impossible, to receive anyone else!

We have to overcome our natural tendency of individualism. I believe most of the experiences in our lives are designed by the enemy to make us ineffective as a united Body of Christ. This is why it is so difficult for us to relate to one another in love. It literally destroys our fellowship with one another. Fellowship is the essence of Biblical Christianity. Fellowship is at the heart of what God uses to grow—not my church, not your church, not America's church, but His Church.

They devoted themselves to the apostles' teaching and to the fellowship, to the breaking of bread and to prayer. Everyone was filled with awe, and many wonders and miraculous signs were done by the apostles...praising God and enjoying the favor of all the people. And the Lord added to their number daily those who were being saved. - Acts 2:42-43, 47

This is the story of the growth of the Christian church. This growth wasn't based on whether or not they spoke in tongues, were Pentecostal or Baptist, sprinkled water on you or whether they immersed. It was the fellowship of the people that God blessed, and the Church was added to daily because they were of one mind. They were not looking at people as outsiders. They were not bigoted, nor was there any partiality of any kind.

The Greek word used in this scripture is koinonia, which translates into "all things in common." That is what we must begin to understand if the Church in America is going to begin to *Cross Colors*.

While all of this speaks to the destructive nature of walls, it is important to acknowledge that some walls do have positive purposes. The example of this is found in the book of Nehemiah. Nehemiah rebuilt the walls around Jerusalem. These walls also served to keep the enemies out.

However, when we look at scriptures we see that there were some subtle, yet very important differences between the walls around Jerusalem and the walls around Jericho. First and foremost, the wall of Jerusalem was a wall that God wanted to be in place. It was a wall that guarded things that God wanted guarded. Also, the wall around Jerusalem allowed for things to come in and out—when it was time.

I said to them, "The gates of Jerusalem are not to be opened until the sun is hot. While the gatekeepers are still on duty, have them shut the doors and bar them. Also appoint residents of Jerusalem as guards, some at their post and some near their own houses." - Nehemiah 7:3

Even though this wall was being rebuilt with enemies within sight of the wall, Nehemiah made provisions that people would be allowed in and out through the gates of the wall. It was done during a specified time and was to be monitored, which is how we should live our lives, carefully monitored. Everyone needs boundaries. Boundaries help us to feel secure. Without them you cannot hope to be emotionally, physically and spiritually healthy. There are people who have no walls at all. They let anything in and anything out. People without boundaries have difficulty respecting themselves for the unique individuals that God made them to be. They want to please everybody and never find out God's purposes for their lives.

To be encased in a solid brick wall with no doors is not good either. The wall of Jericho had one gate, while the wall around

CROSS COLORS: AMERICAN CHRISTIANITY IN BLACK AND WHITE

Jerusalem had ten gates! This shows that Nehemiah had faith in God that they would be protected. The walls in our lives have to be permeable as well. They not only must be solid enough to keep the bad out, but they have to be open enough to let the good in. Unfortunately, we erect walls around our lives that tend to permanently keep everybody out. These walls have got to come down!

Remember the poem written by my church member? They wrote about how they were blessed by someone that they originally were uncertain about letting in. I wish I could tell you how many different ways God's multicultural church has blessed me once I busted some of my walls and crossed colors!

Why do we try to protect ourselves from further hurt, pain or disappointment with walls that ultimately prevent us from receiving many things God wants to give us? I was guilty of this time and time again. It's unfortunate that our natural inclination is to build solid, one gate, Jericho type walls in our lives. Building these walls makes it continually necessary for us to bust a wall.

This is where I was. I asked the Master Builder to help me bust a wall, so that when it was down He could erect the right kind of wall for me. It was really a matter of trust. I had to decide that I could trust God to be my protector, my wall of defense.

God wants good relationships among His people. God wants us to be able to relate in Christian love to each other in spite of our differences, and relate to each other with Him in mind.

For he himself is our peace, who has made the two one and has destroyed the barrier, the dividing wall of hostility. - Ephesians 2:14

I had hope. I had seen God work in my life to free me from other strongholds and walls. I trusted Him. I took the leap of faith that we all must take.

I leaned on my Lord. He gave me words as I stepped out that were appropriate for the moment.

No longer will violence be heard in your land, nor ruin or destruction within your borders, but you will call your walls Salvation and your gates Praise. - Isaiah 60:18

6

❖

How it All Began

*"The trouble is He's lazy. The trouble is He drinks.
The trouble is He's crazy. The trouble is He stinks.
The trouble is He's growing. The trouble is He's grown.
Krupke, we've got troubles of our own.
Please Officer Krupke we're down on our knees.
'Cause no one likes a fella' with a social disease."
- The Jets
(From "West Side Story")*

*"Selfishness originates in blind instinct;
Selfishness blights the germ of all virtue…"
- Alexis de Tocqueville
("Democracy in America")*

I was not born hating whites. However, have no doubt, there was a time when I did hate white folks. I'm not being hyperbolic. This wasn't some misguided mistrust or aggravation; this was an active hate. It was born in pain, and fed throughout my life with steady helpings of prejudice and bigotry from both black and white people.

CROSS COLORS: AMERICAN CHRISTIANITY IN BLACK AND WHITE

Our prejudices generally rise out of our own or someone else's attempt to teach or protect us. We are taught: don't play with fire; don't talk to strangers; put that stick down or you'll poke out someone's eye. As we grow and the world shapes us, we begin developing our own values, standards, and prejudices.

Many times these are rooted in our own comfort, ignorance, and fears. For example, not many young people that I know have a prejudice against television, music, or McDonald's because they grew up watching television, listening to music, and eating McDonalds. They'd have to work pretty hard to develop a prejudice against these things. We develop our mores and values because of how we're socialized. Growing up black in America in the 1950's-60's predetermined that I was going to have a highly tuned antenna toward racial issues.

Here's an example of a situation that in hindsight had more to do with my sin nature than anything else.

I've always been a hustler, so to make money, I would rake leaves, shovel snow, or cut somebody's grass, for black and white families. It made no difference to me who I worked for because the only color that I was concerned about at that time was green. I just wanted to get paid. They all encouraged me and called me industrious. They wanted the work done right, and I worked hard to make sure it was. None of them was patronizing me or giving me a hand out; they paid me for my work. The white families usually paid more for their lawns, so you can imagine who I went to first.

Now, brothers that are caught up in the paranoia and deceit of the Nation of Islam would tell you that this was the "blue eyed devil" sowing the seeds of self-hatred and setting the standard for catering to whites at an early age. By using the fact that whites tended to have more money to pay me than my black brothers and sisters, I would ultimately have more respect and love for the "blond-blue-eyed devil" than I would for my own black brothers and sisters, and ultimately for myself.

That's the white man's ploy. That's how the white devil works, my brother.

People caught up in the left-wing politics of so-called socialism and communism would tell me that this was an example of the capitalist indoctrination: the bourgeoisie capitalist establishment subliminally telling me that they control the purse strings and that proletariats like me are and will continue to be their workers.

Fight against it, my African American brother—revolt!

The right wing would tell me that this was nothing more than good ol' God-loving American values at work. America is a capitalist society, and I was learning at an early age the importance of doing a good job, and the importance of pointing myself toward the right market. That was nothing but the American dream in action.

Rugged individualism, my boy. You work hard and pull yourself up by your own bootstraps, and you'll be compensated for it. Succeed in this country, and be a credit to your race.

Black power/left wing/right wing politics—an unholy trinity that flourished in the African American community in the 1960's and is still claiming lives today. They have been three very strong influences in my life, whether or not I was with them or against them. Now, I know I'm the only person that this has ever happened to, but I have at different times in my life allowed this triple-threat to overshadow the influence of God on my life. These other influences appeal to our fears, our unbelief and selfishness.

In hindsight, I realized that the counsel of godly people would have convicted me of my sin of selfishness and greed. They would have reminded me to work as if I was working for God. They would say to me that it shouldn't have made any difference who paid me if, as we sing, "I woke up in the morning with my mind stayed on Jesus." But this was not the counsel that I sought or heard at that time.

But how do you keep that godly focus when you're treated as less than human on a regular basis?

How do you do it when you are told that those people are dangerous and that you should stay away from them?

How do you do it when you never come into contact with these people in a situation of trust and love?

Impossible? So it would seem. And so it seemed to me.

Partiality works to destroy God's creation. Its ultimate goal is to destroy everyone that it comes in contact with: white or black, rich or poor, it makes no difference. This is a disease that affects all that are involved with it, no matter which side of the color line you happen to be on. In this country, we all become indoctrinated into this spirit of partiality and racism, without even realizing it.

My family always related to white people. As long as I can remember, whites visited our home. Our family was poor when I was growing up. My parents were also in the ministry. The ministry that God had given them wasn't bringing in a lot of money, so white Christians were always bringing food, clothing or money to our house. My parents didn't "suck up" to them; some of these people were their close friends. When I say "suck up" I mean that they weren't just patronizing them when they told them "thank you," or praying with them when they came by because they were bringing gifts. They were in relationships with many of them and the friendships were genuine.

It was embarrassing sometimes, however. Other kids didn't have white people bringing stuff to their house and sometimes we were teased about it.

Hey, welfare ain't good enough for y'all? You got to have your own personal white folks bringing y'all food!

What kinda' clothes did you get this week?

I understood it though. I realized some of the kids that teased us were jealous.

Don't get me wrong—all the white folks who came by our house and who we dealt with weren't friends though. Many of them were just doing what they did out of wrong and patronizing motives. These were the ones that I began to categorize as "phony white folks."

As I grew up, I began to understand that some whites were just patronizing. They wanted a badge for helping the underprivileged—us po' coloreds that wuz sufferin' so much.

Is you goan' hep' us, massah'?

"Come on you poor, dumb, little black child, and let me help you."

No one ever said this out loud, but many times I sensed it in their attitudes or the way they treated me. It was as if they would slum for a while, help us out, and then run back to their big WHITE houses and say: *"See Lord? I'm obedient; I'm helping them,"* and then go wash themselves as quickly as they could. I never liked it when I was treated that way. From this point on, I began to look at white folks a little differently.

When you grow up being treated a certain way, you begin to develop a knack for telling who's real and who's phony. You begin to see what real Christian love is, and what is just an act that they use to try to convince themselves that they are living like Christians.

I began to see it in some of the people who brought things to our house to help us. I also could tell which teachers in my school were sick of us little nappy-headed kids. They looked down on us and didn't think we were as smart as the white children were. Although I had some teachers that were just the opposite and who were very sensitive, and not all of the whites that came to our house were like that, their difference was not enough to melt the hatred growing inside me. I began laying down my foundation for the wall.

In hindsight, I find it amazing how we allow a very vocal minority to jade the way we look at the majority of people, but that is the nature of sin. We can easily remember the few people who caused us pain, but our memories tend to fade at the thought of all the people who have benefited our lives.

As my parents continued to get more involved in ministry, we started to go to Christian camps. Every summer, our family would participate in the Detroit Rescue Mission camp. Many of the children who participated in this camp were from destitute, hurting situations. These children's parents may have been substance abusers or prostitutes, and the camp was set up to get them out of the city and away from that environment, if only for one week out of a year.

The Cross children, however, were not in that group. We were the children of the leaders in the camp. Yet it never failed that the counselors put us all in the same bag—The Ghetto. These were phony white folks, using phony liberalism to be phony Christians.

Patronizing and treating us in condescending ways, they addressed us as "you people".

They talked down to us.

"You people ought to be grateful."

"If it weren't for us, you'd be going to hell."

"If it weren't for us, you people wouldn't have a camp."

"If it weren't for us...'

This was at a Christian camp! I remember thinking:

"If it weren't for YOU, I wouldn't hate all white folks!"

"Is this the only camp available for poor and underprivileged black kids?" *"Why do they have all the money, ideas, schools, and nice facilities?"*

"Why did we always seem to be on the bottom?"

"Why were we always receiving a hand out?"

"Why didn't black people have their own camps and facilities?"

"Why were we always at the mercy of white people—phony white folks at that?"

No one seemed to be able to give me a decent answer to my questions, and even if they had, I doubt that I would have accepted it. So the hatred inside me continued to grow, and I began stacking the bricks and mortar that would make up my wall.

In the fourth grade, I had a white teacher, Mrs. D., whom I liked. I'll always remember that she read "Les Miserables" to us. It was a novel about a French guy who was the underdog but eventually came out on top. She read it in an attempt to encourage us. By choosing this book, she was communicating to us that we were intelligent enough to handle an adult classic. She was a champion of the underdog. She believed that if people in society believed in us, then we could achieve.

It was a great blessing to have her as a teacher and having her read the novel to us was a very positive experience for me. Yet, because of the wall that I was building, I looked at her as one of the very few who cared, out of the many who absolutely did not.

By the time I was in the fourth grade, I had already begun to determine that most, if not all, white folks didn't have my or any other black person's best interest at heart.

Even good experiences with whites were not able to knock down any of the bricks I had formed. Once again, I was a victim of the nature of the walls. They are so impenetrable that in keeping out the bad, they also hinder anything good from coming in.

I was nine years old, it was 1958, and the civil rights movement was beginning to take shape in the South. In Detroit you could feel people begin to draw battle lines.

I was no different. I continued to build the wall around my heart.

7

❖

Finding Out the Truth

*"People movin' out. People movin' in. Why?
Because of the color of our skin."
- The Temptations
("Ball of Confusion")*

*"I guess it is easy for those who have never felt the stinging darts of segregation to say wait. But when you have seen vicious mobs lynch your mothers and fathers at will… When you have to concoct an answer for a 5 year old son asking in agonizing pathos: 'Daddy, why do white people treat colored people so mean?'… When your first name becomes nigger and your middle name becomes boy (however old you are) then you will understand why we find it difficult to wait."
- Dr. Martin Luther King, Jr.
("Letter from Birmingham Jail")*

CROSS COLORS: AMERICAN CHRISTIANITY IN BLACK AND WHITE

BOOM! Men were flying into outer space!
BOOM!!! We almost went to war with Cuba and Russia.
BOOM!!! Guys were getting drafted to go fight in a place called Vietnam (I had no idea where that was).

BOOM!!! Black folks were marching and demanding their civil rights.

BOOM!!! Black folks were all over the news, saying things that I had never heard them say:

"You didn't land on Plymouth Rock! Plymouth Rock landed on YOU!"

"I will no longer be answering to the name Cassius Clay; my name is now Muhammed Ali."

"I have a Dream..."

That's how it hit me! BOOM!!! The 60's hit, the world was in a turmoil, and all this black awareness stuff exploded on the scene.

I was a Christian at Detroit Northern High School at the time. I was supportive of the Church. I wanted to stand up strong for Christianity, but then I heard about how white people had used the Church for their own gains and how they distorted it to justify the kidnapping and keeping of slaves. The truth hurts, and when I began to discover some of history of the Church, especially the church in America, I felt so betrayed. I really began to accelerate setting up my walls.

The black nationalists and the Nation of Islam were targeting the Church with some serious indictments and bringing out facts I had never heard. They talked about how white Christians had participated in the slave trade and how they had manipulated the Scriptures during the years of American slavery to keep blacks docile and in chains. What?!

Yeah my brother. They got you sitting up there praying to a blond blue-eyed white Jesus, who ain't 'bout to do nuthin' for you. You better off praying to Santa Claus!

Brother, don't you know that all those fathers of our country that were supposed to be Christian were all actually slave owners?

And these same "Christians" came over here and either stole or killed the Indians for their land. Gave them diseases like small pox and murdered their women and children.

Just like they did to us.

I was pissed. I got angry. How could they do that? Why didn't someone in the Church talk about this? Why didn't someone tell me? How could THEY withhold the truth from us all that time?

I was angry already, so it wasn't long before I became as radical as the black nationalists and the Nation of Islam brothers.

I wanted to do something about segregation/bigotry/racism—or whatever it was being called that week—so I got involved with anything that was radical or was against the white establishment.

One of the most memorable things I was involved with was staging a walk out in our high school. The whole school walked out. We even walked over to the neighborhood junior high school and coerced them to walk out too. Our entire school shut down for a month. That feeling of strength, power and total disregard for THEIR rules was intoxicating! All the things that had been said and done to me by phony white folks over the years took a back seat to the new-found feeling of power that I got from that. It was as if I had finally said to all of them: *There! What do you think of that! If it weren't for YOU, this school wouldn't be shut down!*

The feeling of power that I got from rebelling was not only intoxicating but was addictive as well, just like a drug. That power felt good when you lived in a society that let you know in no uncertain terms that you were not valued. Every person wants and needs to know, or at least think, that they are valued. Growing up black in this society didn't afford me many situations that promoted a feeling of value.

I relate easily to the kids of today who worship athletes like LeBron James, Dwyane Wade or Michael Jordan. In my day, it was men like Willie Mays, Hank Aaron and Muhammad Ali. You want to be like them because of the value that is placed on their abilities. African American sports stars throughout history have been some of the few people of our race who were valued in our society. This is why so many of our children run toward sports and entertainment instead of academia. They want their lives to have a sense of value. Since historically we have not been valued for our mental capabilities, we find somewhere else to get our esteem.

The drug of rebellion led me toward actively hating everything that I defined as the white establishment. I detested the white establishment of this country during the sixties. For me it became more than just some nebulous entity that disregarded me and my people—this included my absolute being and existence.

For me, the white establishment became tangible and alive; it became known as "The Man." "The Man" embodied everything that I hated or feared about whites and this country in general. "The Man" was a living, breathing organism that was against me and wanted to destroy me.

"The Man" was:

A government that allowed my people to be lynched and murdered while the perpetrators walked free.

A red-necked sheriff that turned fire hoses and dogs loose on civil rights marchers.

A coward who ran around beneath a white sheet and burned crosses and bombed churches.

"Christian" camp counselors who said things like: "If it weren't for your people..."

The unvalued and disenfranchised have used different drugs to combat, escape or narcotize their simultaneous fear and hatred of "The Man." Some of us used the drug of power that we experienced from rebelling.

After feeling powerless for so long, when you were able to gain even a little power over something, you craved it, and wanted to keep that feeling going. Interrupting the teacher lead to disrupting class, which led to disrupting school. Rebelling against parents would lead to rebelling against teachers.

I began looking at the teachers and the types of things they were doing. I looked at how many black teachers were not really on our side but were black "wanna' be's." I became very resentful about what I observed around me.

In response, I also became *black!* That was a prescription that came straight from Dr. Feelgood for many of us! I was no longer colored, and I wasn't about to be called Negro—NO WAY—you better make sure you call me BLACK!

I was listening to albums with Malcolm X speeches and wearing a big 'fro. I just jumped into being militant with both feet—it was fun.

It really shook my parents up, because at the same time that their son, Haman Jr., was walking around looking and acting like Huey Newton and the rest of the Black Panthers, they had really moved forward with their ministry. This was their ministry that got a lot of support from whites! It got to the point where they eventually had to change the name of their ministry because of pressure from militant blacks. Originally, it was called Detroit's Little Africa. That sounded way too white for all of us who were out in the streets. It was changed and still is called Afro American Mission.

The guys that I hung out with at school were some serious thinkers. There were atheists, philosophers and some were just flat out "hoods" who had some brains. If you can imagine gangsta-philosophers, that's who I was hanging with. We never had a black history class; we were getting our information from all kinds of sources. Quite a few white teachers who were communists supported us in our militancy. They were giving us a lot of information about the way segregation and racism worked within and throughout the systems of the government.

It was a lot of good ammunition and it helped strengthen the platform that we were standing on whenever we wanted to influence other students or just get people riled up. The more I learned, the angrier I got. Pretty soon I was screaming about the plight of the Black Man in the Ghetto, and telling people that the white man was the enemy.

Because these brothers that I hung out with where either leaning toward being in the Nation of Islam, or just atheists, we would talk religion a lot. They were always talking about how the worst thing for black people in America was the Church. It brainwashed them, made them docile, easy targets for the white man, and was just another way to keep us in bondage. It was really stimulating for me, arguing and debating with these guys, because in the midst of it I was strengthening my knowledge of the Word.

They could never understand why I defended the Church the way I did. A few of them would dismiss me as having been too brainwashed by white folks. Sometimes after hearing some of my views, I think they actually wondered how I could be black, grow up in the ghetto and still think that way?

I didn't really care what they thought. I was a lot of things at that time, but I still loved God and was trying to work out why the things that were going on in my life were going on. Turn my back on God? I wasn't going to be that big of a fool. I still knew the truth of God's Word even if I wasn't walking in it, or was too caught up in the politics of the world to allow the Word to act out through me. So when they would talk this smack, I defended the Word.

The rage of the '60's proved to be a very convenient outlet for my anger. It was something I could do to get back at white folks. I was still a Christian, I still professed to love Christ, but now I had a few other adjectives preceding it.

Hi. I'm Haman Cross, Jr., a youngBLACKmilitantChristianman.

Then I found out that the most segregated hour of the week in America occurred on Sunday mornings at 11:00 a.m. I had just been angry with white folks prior to that, but now that gave way to anger, bitterness and blazing hatred.

The most segregated hour has not changed in the last 50 years either. All around this great country of ours, from Monday through Friday, blacks and whites go to work together—whether it was imposed on them by the government or not. We will go out and bowl in leagues, play on softball teams, and watch the latest movies in the same theater. All of this we will do together. Yet, in a country that considers itself a Christian nation, black and whites will not worship together.

This is the most important thing that we can do as believers and we won't do it together.

I wanted to be involved and do something about partiality and prejudice against black people. I felt it was at least the Christian thing to do, but I was so disappointed with the response of the Church.

The absence of white Christians in the civil rights movement bothered me. They would claim that the response of the Church was the entire social gospel—no other response was needed. No other response had a place in the church; that's politics, not Christianity. You hear virtually the same message from many evangelicals today; the only way to solve this problem is through getting people to make a decision for Christ! But I ask you, if people feel like you don't care about their well-being in society, how are you going to present the Gospel to them effectively, let alone get them to make a decision for Christ?

Black Christian musicians of the '60's, such as Andre Crouch, were considered too worldly. To the Church, anything black or with a beat was dark, evil and from Satan. The Church seemed to have the attitude that said:

"Yes Lord, let us be the light of the world and the salt of the

earth for the sinners. But just make sure that they are the sinners that live where we live, look like we look, and talk just like we talk. And oh yeah God, make sure that they know that we love them, even though we don't want to be around them. Couldya' do that?"

I just got tired of all the hypocrisy.

Many of the black evangelical, fundamental churches did not know how to address the questions that were being raised. Many of the black Christian churches and Christian organizations were funded by white people, and it looked as though they just didn't want to ask the hard questions and run the risk of having their funding pulled from them. My attitude was, "We don't need you or your money. You are all messed up."

I recall an experience I had in college. Detroit Bible College decided to move from the city in the 70's. The neighborhood was changing and as a result of the riots in the '60's, white flight occurred. White homeowners, businesses, churches, and now the college joined the bandwagon. About 15-20 black students challenged the president. We took over his office. He argued that staying in the city would hinder the school's progress. In other words, they wanted white students to come and feel safe. We also found out that the school was supporting a camp that black children could not attend. We brought these matters of racism to their attention. But our comments made no difference—the school still moved.

Accepting the reality of partiality among Christians hurt tremendously. My desire and intention was to write them off like other whites. To facilitate this, I went to The Book of Excuses, and turned to the chapter that I was editing.

1 Patrick 6:65—"They are all the same."
Bigotry 3:1—"It doesn't matter if they are Christians."
Bigotry 5:8 —"They're ALL prejudiced."
1 Patrick 4:23—"They are all scared of us."
Songs of Stupidity—"There's not a true Christian among them."

I had enough bricks and mortar now that my positive experiences with whites were completely overshadowed.

I couldn't understand why God would say He loved me, yet allow these people to mistreat my people. These same people, who would treat us like dirt, were running Christian camps where we all held hands and sang songs like "Jesus Loves the Little Children!"

It felt so wrong, like everybody was just lying. I wanted so much to "hate white folks for Jesus." That would have made me feel better. That would have made sense to my walled-over heart. That would have taken away some of the pain. Yet the contradiction in terms was just too obvious. It didn't ease any of the pain or anger that I was feeling.

The discovery of my people being mistreated by another race of people fueled my anger to the boiling point. Without considering God or His desire for my life, I erected all my walls. I became very proficient at building walls. For years, I worked feverishly to build and fortify my bastion.

If white people want it that way, that's what they are gonna' get.

I thought I was protecting myself from further pain.

I hate white people...a brick, *I hate white people*...some mortar, *I hate...*

Like most people who build walls, I didn't realize that I was perpetuating my pain. But that's exactly what happens. You're building higher, wider, and stronger walls but you are trapping yourself inside of this wall with all of your fear, anger, and pain. You are literally encasing yourself inside a wall with the devil and shutting God out.

God can't get through to speak a word of truth to you, because Satan is busy telling you lies and you honestly weren't trying to listen to God anyway. Satan continues to work on you until he gets you to put yourself in situations that will increase your fear, anger, and pain.

I would go to meetings with my parents knowing that we would be the only blacks there, which would increase my anger. In these Christian circles, since I was the only black youth who attended the meetings, I was determined I would be the tough guy. I came in with a chip on my shoulder and I would sit and glare at people.

Look at these phony white folks! I can't stand you!

Boy, wouldn't it be nice to let them feel how black people felt? I wondered how they would like it if somebody just tossed a bomb into their church, if somebody lynched one of their relatives. Would it be so easy for them to walk around and act like they loved us then?

I went from being Haman Cross, Jr., THE NEGRO AVENGER to Haman Cross, Jr. SUPER BLACK NIGGER! I didn't want to sound, dress or act anything like a white boy. I used Black English whenever I spoke to them.

"Why, Haman how are you? I haven't seen you in a long time."

I'm cool homes. Dig, I can't rap wit' choo' right now 'cause I gotta book. But you stay cool, awright? Yeah.

They call it Ebonics these days, but whatever it was, I tried to make them feel like they didn't know anything about me. There were only a couple of things that I wanted them to know about me, and I gave them these impressions all the time:

I was a mad, angry, and dangerous nigger to be near.

That this dangerous nigger could beat up five of them at one time.

I would get my respect by being mean and intimidating. Those were the things that building the walls had taught me.

I knew the Bible well, so when I went to these meetings I would challenge and correct them, and make the leaders look stupid. I could tell by the looks on their faces that they were thinking, "Nig... Blacks kids are not supposed to know this stuff. Especially nig... black kids who look and act like him."

It was a game. Being the smart tough guy was a way to get back at them for having so much power and control over me and my people. I put on this act to keep people from knowing how insecure and unsure of myself I really was. And I continued to build those walls of self-protection, anger, bitterness—you name it. I was adding to my walls the bricks and mortar needed to keep them growing higher and higher.

After high school, I went to Nyack College in New York. It was a predominantly white school where I couldn't compete with the other students. They talked about chemistry, which I didn't take in high school. They all had educational and financial advantages over me. Instead of focusing on who I was and WHOSE I was, I just became embarrassed, angrier and more jealous.

I dealt with my anger by becoming SUPER DUPER BLACK NIGGER.

Because of my Bible background and all the things that I had learned in the last few years, I would argue with all of the professors. And, I would turn everything into an issue of race. They call it "playing the race card" now, but I just wanted to let people know that all this stuff that they were trying to overlook, sugar-coat, and homogenize was real.

If you want to call that playing the race card, well, I played that baby all the time. I would ask questions like: "Why don't you have more black teachers and students here?"

Missionaries from the Christian Missionary Alliance would come in and I would say: *"You've been in African countries for 100 years and the people are still poor and ragged. Whatchoo doin' down there?"* The professors and administrators hated to see me coming.

I was hanging out with the wildest guys I could find; the ones who were basically renegades. It was a Christian college, but I found the closest thing there was to a hippie on that campus to hang out with. I found I had a lot in common with these guys, the most important of which was that we were all mad. Mad at the world, mad at the government, mad at the war—you name it, we were mad about it. The white boys that I was hanging out with were so anti-establishment, they would even talk about "the white man keeping people down." They all identified with my venom. Besides our anger, we were all into carnality as well.

There were no black girls at the college so I just went after all the white girls that I could. The white boys were cool with me until I started to mess with the white girls. I thought to myself, "Your white girls want me and I'm going to take them out and get all in your face with them." I was never serious about any of them; I was just using them to get back at white people. I knew they couldn't stand to see Haman Cross, Jr., SUPER DUPER BLACK NIGGER, with their white women. I had a lot of anger and this was one way I could have power over them. I made sure they knew that I wasn't walking around being "just friends" with them either. The white boys knew what was up, and I made sure that they got to see me with the white girls as often as I could.

I probably would not have gone so far out there with the white women if I had been able to play basketball, but the coach was making sure that I got no playing time. I rode the bench because of my grades, and when it wasn't that, I rode the bench because I was black.

There is one thing that I love to do and that is win. I love to win at everything I ever get involved with. Playing golf, playing basketball, coaching basketball, fights, fighting partiality or fighting the devil—I have to WIN! Playing basketball would have helped me vent some venom through the pure competitiveness, but I wasn't even allowed to do that.

I got kicked out during my second year in college.

My behavior, attitude and academics were not acceptable. I didn't show much Christianity in me at all at the time. I was way—WAY—out there. And way out of fellowship with God—BIG TIME.

I reacted to the realities of partiality by erecting huge walls of anger and bitterness. Unfortunately, walls of anger and bitterness keep us from relating to others as Christ would have us relate to them. Again, we cannot always prevent the bad things that happen to us, but we do have a responsibility to bust a wall when God shows us that we have built them.

Though we build all kinds of walls in our lives, I soon discovered that there are no walls quite like the walls against authority and walls of self-rejection.

8

❖

Walls Against Rejection and Walls of Self-Rejection

"Braving obstacles and hardships is nobler than retreat to tranquility. The butterfly that hovers around the lamp until it dies is more admirable than the mole that lives in a dark tunnel."
- Kahlil Gibran

"I am an invisible man. No, I am not a spook like those who haunted Edgar Allan Poe; nor am I one of your Hollywood movie ectoplasms. I am a man of substance, of flesh and bone, fiber and liquids—and I might even be said to possess a mind. I am invisible, understand, simply because people refuse to see me. Like the bodiless heads you see sometimes in circus sideshows, it is as though I have been surrounded by mirrors of hard, distorting glass. When they approach me they see only my surroundings, themselves, or figments of their imagination—indeed, everything and anything except me."
- Ralph Ellison
("Invisible Man")

OmyGod! What am I gonna' do now?!

That's all I could think of when what I had done finally sunk in. I had never thought I would get kicked out of school. As crazy as I had acted, school was something that I thought would always be there for me. My life was like a lot of people's lives. Monday through Friday you went to school. Saturday was a free day. And on Sunday you went to church. Five days of my life had just been turned upside down for me.

OmyGod! What am I gonna' do now?!

Up until that time, all my stuff—even though it felt real—was still like a game. But getting kicked out of school let me know that there are consequences to actions. I don't think I had really considered the potential consequences. Being on the basketball team but not getting any "tick" was a bad experience, but I was always able to dismiss it as the coach being prejudiced. I couldn't change the fact that I was black, so that was something I had no control over.

I never considered the idea that my behavior—something that I could control—was a reason that I didn't get on the court. I figured that I would act a fool, get my degree, go out into the workforce, make my money, and continue to trip out all along the way.

Getting kicked out of school woke me up.

And it forced me to face the fact that I wasn't just some innocent victim in this whole thing. All the anger, bitterness and animosity wasn't just one-sided. I looked back over the last two years of my life and was disgusted. When you act like I did, it becomes pretty clear that you don't like very many people.

This situation I now found myself in now forced me to look into the mirror every morning and realize that I didn't really like the person staring back at me. That hurt. Putting blame and excuse for failure on someone else is easy, but when you've run out of scapegoats and have to face yourself, you realize that since you can't teach yourself something that you don't know, you need help. Facing my problems and myself head on was the catalyst that led me to rededicate my life to God. In rededicating myself to God, I was then able to make some progress in my life.

Years later, when I began to *Cross Colors*, the same steps that I took for growth out of my self-destructive and self-rejecting attitude that I had as a young man, were the steps that I needed to retrace as an older man.

I did not like who I was. The paradox was that before I could shed my shell, I had to accept it. If we are not happy with our own ethnic differences, it's difficult to appreciate someone else's. That issue would come out later for me. Before I could do anything, I had to work on the fact that because I didn't like or love who I was, there was going to be no way that I could truly like or love anyone else, especially God. That list also included wife, children, friends, neighbors, parents, strangers, dogs… You get the idea.

I didn't like being Haman Cross, Jr. In wishing to be different—which is essentially what I was guilty of in resenting my identity—I was making the statement to God that I could see no benefit in how He made me or where He'd placed me.

A person who rejects the way God designed him will often manipulate others. Self-rejection can manifest itself in a domineering, controlling, "I must be in charge" attitude. This individual often forfeits his freedom in self-acceptance, and lives in resignation—bound to an unbiblical and misguided opinion of themselves. This person feels, "I must be in charge of my life and all who impact my life." Of course, this attitude hinders loving relationships.

One of the members of Rosedale Park Baptist Church related a pretty typical story to me about his supervisor. The supervisor would frequently usurp tasks that he had delegated, rather than give employees an opportunity to learn and master a task. This behavior was very demeaning to his coworkers. It communicated to them that they could never get it right, but he, on the other hand, could always "handle it." This type of control is a vain attempt to elevate oneself. When we really appreciate God's sovereignty and His ability to make us exactly the way He wanted us, we don't feel compelled to denigrate and ridicule someone else to elevate ourselves.

Often the bully of the classroom is the boy who is conspicuously short or very poor. Or perhaps he's overweight or really tall for his age. The more unique a person's appearance, the more he tends to be self-conscious. Teasing and taunting someone else is actually a vain attempt to divert ridicule about one's own uniqueness.

I was very unique. I knew the Bible. I had values and ideals like most middle-class whites. Yet I came from poverty. White Christians had rejected me because of the color of my skin. I could identify with angry blacks who were tired of the double standards. I was angry and bitter. No one else appreciated who I was, and I came to agree with my detractors. White people didn't like me; I was too black. Black people didn't like me; I was too white.

Why did God make me this way? Why did God give me this shell? I was filled with resentment toward God for being born black, poor, and a minister's son.

There are some people who theorize that the personality that rejects self and constructs these kinds of walls has low self-esteem. I can see this, but I think there is more to this than just low self-esteem. I think this sort of rejection is also evident in a person who is very self-absorbed: "I can't. They hurt me. I'm too short…too dark…I want…" You get the idea. A person who is so self-absorbed is usually fragile, vulnerable, and dangerous. That described me to a T. Does anybody else see themselves in this picture?

I was fragile because I had felt unprotected for most of my life, beginning in my childhood. I felt that I had not been cared for as a child. This led me to erect a wall against authority. Since my parents were the authority figures that I felt had done nothing to protect me, I felt I couldn't trust anyone in authority to care for me at all.

All children need parental attention and companionship. When parents are not available because of wrong priorities or personal problems, children begin to struggle with feelings of unimportance and unworthiness. Parents are supposed to nurture and protect their children. Most desire to. Sometimes the zeal to do well as parents gets lost in other demands or overwhelming problems that distract moms and dads, regardless of their good intentions.

As a child, I had legitimate needs, and for many years I felt like those needs meant nothing to my father. My father was a pastor who was very involved in his ministry. This is something that all Christians must look at with an eye of self-examination. The question must always be asked: Am I taking care of my first ministry—my family?

Since my parents were in the ministry, they were always helping someone else's child. At a very early age, I began to build a wall to protect myself from what I thought was my dad's rejection of me, since I felt that he never had enough time for me. I hated never spending time with my father. He didn't even come to any of my basketball games!

What about me? When are you gonna' be there for ME?!!! What do I have to do to get your attention?!

When I didn't get attention from my father (positive or negative) I built a wall against authority. They (authority figures) aren't here to love you; they're just there to be an authority. Every day the wall got bigger and bigger. I decided that I wouldn't care. I became callous, hard, bitter.

I don't really need him...

This last thought, too, has shaped a lot of decisions I've made in life, and many of those decisions have been bad ones (they probably all have but I don't want to think about all of them right now). I can tell you without a doubt that I have suffered the consequences of building that wall more than I care to think about. Walls against authority are quite dangerous, because they have to do with true love and submission. If we fight and refuse to submit to earthly authority, there is no way that we will truly submit to God, our heavenly father and authority.

Obey your leaders and submit to their authority. They keep watch over you as men who must give an account. Obey them so that their work will be a joy, not a burden, for that would be of no advantage to you. - Hebrews 13:17

Submit yourselves for the Lord's sake to every authority instituted among men: whether to the king, as the supreme authority. - 1 Peter 2:13

Young men, in the same way be submissive to those who are older. All of you, clothe yourselves with humility toward one another, because God opposes the proud but gives grace to the humble. - 1 Peter 5:5

If anyone says, "I love God," yet hates his brother, he is a liar. For anyone who does not love his brother, whom he has seen, cannot love God, whom he has not seen. - 1 John 4:20

I had to look over those scriptures again and again, meditating on them because I had such a huge wall against authority. I realized that I didn't make raising me any bed of roses for my parents, even with all my excuses—real or imagined—that I had ready and waiting to use.

Many of us do this same thing unconsciously. We don't realize that because our parents are our first and primary authority figures, we are making our lives difficult simply because we do not recognize this wall for the huge sin that it is. I know that with me, I just thought of it as something that I had against my parents.

"No big deal, it's just the culture and times that I'm growing up in."

"It's easy—too easy for children to think that same thought."

"It's just a generation gap."

"My mom and dad just aren't hip."

"My old Girl ain't up with what's down."

"My old Dude just ain't down with wassup."

You probably have your own way of saying it, but the sad fact is that it has to do with building walls against authority, which is not submitting, and that is ultimately not loving.

Submitting means to yield or surrender oneself to the will or authority of another. This is something that as children we just feel we shouldn't do, especially if our needs aren't being met. I had my wall against authority set in place and had all my reasons and rationales for it being there. *My father wasn't this... My father wasn't there when... My mother didn't do this for me when...*

They were all there, all the excuses we can use when we get on the talk shows and tell everyone across the country: this is why I acted this way or that. What we should really be saying is this: the reason I acted a fool is because I didn't want to submit and ultimately love, even though that's what God told me to do.

Children, obey your parents in the Lord, for this is right. Honor your father and mother—which is the first commandment with a promise—that it may go well with you and that you may enjoy long life on the earth. - Ephesians 6:1-3

This commandment does not tell us to honor our parents conditionally. It does not say honor your father and mother... IF! We are to do this because it is commanded of us, not by our earthly father, but by our Heavenly Father. The commandment even has a promise, "that it may go well with you and that you may enjoy long life on the earth."

I had to learn this and I must admit I learned it a lot later than I would have liked. This is a promise that all children should know, because it is absolutely true. I laughed about it when I was younger, but once I had children of my own I realized why my father would say things like "Boy, I'm the one that brought you here. I can take you away from here too!" Whenever my father said that, I straightened up and started obeying, submitting, whatever he wanted me to do, because I wanted to "enjoy long life on the earth." So did my children.

The Bible is full of stories of people with walls against authority. Begin with the fall of Satan from heaven, and the fall of man from the Garden. So don't shrug your shoulders and ask, "Who me? I don't have a problem with authority." The Bible shows us that we do this naturally.

Once we learn submission and begin to learn to love, we break down the wall against authority. The wall against authority must have the spirit of the lack of submission to stand on. Once we learn submission, it crumbles and falls. That's it. It has nothing else to stand on.

I don't know exactly about why your wall against authority was built, I can only tell you that if you have a problem crossing colors— YOU HAVE ONE.

Submitting to God's authority will bust down that wall against authority, and begin to enable you to trust and have security in Him more.

Once we begin to trust Him more, we can then begin to trust and love ourselves; who God made us to be. In order to Cross Colors and be comfortable with persons of various and different colors, we must find security in who God has created us to be.

The second is this: 'Love your neighbor as yourself.' There is no commandment greater than these. - Mark 12:31

Simply put: you gotta' love yourself before you can love anybody else.

Accepting God's design is simply accepting the unchangeable aspects of our identity over which we have no control. We've all seen the little posters of the child staring back and saying, "I know I'm somebody, 'cause God don't make no junk!" This is true. God lovingly ordained all the personal features that make us uniquely who we are long before we were born! Acceptance of this busts the wall of self-rejection. I had to learn to accept myself as I understood God's design and acceptance of me. Sometimes we feel God made a mistake in making us, but God does not make mistakes. Let me repeat that: God does not make mistakes. It's up to us to learn that we are just what God wants us to be. I had to realize that I am a designer's original.

"And now, saith the LORD that formed me from the womb to be his servant to bring Jacob again to him, Though Israel be not gath-

ered, yet shall I be glorious in the eyes of the LORD, and my God shall be my strength. - Isaiah 49:5 (KJV)

It is not unusual for a black person to wish at some point in his/her life that they had not been born black, particularly in America. This may also be true for other races.

Probably less common are whites that wish they were another color. But I'm sure it happens. We all want to be different than we are. But, to reject God's design makes us worthy of His rebuke.

But who are you, O man, to talk back to God? Shall what is formed say to him who formed it, 'Why did you make me like this?' Does not the potter have the right to make out of the same lump of clay some pottery for noble purposes and some for common use? - Romans 9:20-21

For we are God's workmanship, created in Christ Jesus to do good works, which God prepared in advance for us to do. - Ephesians 2:10

The Greek word for workmanship is poiema, which means "a work or art, a product that is designed." Each unchangeable aspect of my identity was strategically and carefully chosen by God to bring to pass His perfect purposes for my life! Your purpose—the one that God has for you, not the one that you think or WANT for your life—might be so far from what you can conceive, or what you are comfortable with that you may be shocked when God presents it to you. It is for you, however. It's not being invented for someone else. The things that we go through in life are all a part of that workmanship. This is how God presented a call on my life.

When I was a kid, Highland Park Baptist Church in Highland Park, Michigan sponsored a camp and one of my buddies and I got to go. It was a serious "back to nature" camp. While we were there, we lived like we were out in the jungle—you know, no toilets, no cabins, cooking over open fires—really forcing all of us from the city out of our comfort zones. I liked it though. It really got me focused on God. It also gave the counselors an opportunity to give us some serious insight into what some mission fields might be like. The counselors kept emphasizing that it was very important that my buddy (who was also black), and I should become missionaries. That had never really occurred to me. All of the missionaries I had ever known were white.

Become a missionary? Go out and spread God's Word to Africa,

South America, and other far off places? Black people, poor people; we were the victims. Weren't the missionaries supposed to come out to us? Here I was, a black kid who was born and raised in the inner city, out here in the woods and these counselors were sweating me about going out into the mission field. I was more concerned about where I was going to use the bathroom before I went to sleep that night. How was I going to spread God's Word in the jungles of this world?

Who am I? What do I have to offer to anybody? Who was I? What did I have that was important to contribute? Wait a minute. Is that a snake over there?

That's what was going through my mind. Yet, the longer the camp went on, the more the counselors emphasized my importance on the mission field. God had obviously prompted their hearts, because they were dogged about this. I began to sense God's call on my life. It was during this camp that I told the Lord that I would be a missionary. I would make myself available not only to be used by Him, but also to just "go." And not just to Africa; if He wanted me to go to another culture even though I was black, I'd be willing to do that. This camp was not just an emotional experience. I truly made a firm commitment to God's call. It was a life-changing experience. It's this commitment and the grace that God supplies that I have drawn on when things have gotten rough, and believe me, I have seen rough.

Little did I know that God did want me to minister to a culture that was different from mine, except that I wouldn't have to travel, buy an airline ticket or passport to minister to another culture. I wouldn't have to physically "go" anywhere! Emotionally and spiritually traveling and growing would be another issue, however. There are times, believe me, when I feel like it would probably have been easier to go to Africa—maybe even Mars—than to answer the call to minister across the color lines here in America!

That's what God was preparing me for throughout my entire life. Even though I accepted the call out in the jungle, He was busy working to make me someone who could also serve Him in the urban jungle, the suburban jungle, and the jungle of privilege.

I now realize that God allowed me the many experiences that came with being a black male, raised in a minister's home, living in poverty, growing up in a society that thinks of me as public enemy number one, to shape me. He used the realities of racism that I experienced to shape me. Yes, He even used the pain. Pain and everything else had its purpose in God's plan for my life.

As an adult, I attended two very significant conferences that impacted my life. The first was a Bill Gothard conference. For the first time, I understood the reason God made me black. I began to accept my physical features. I didn't feel the need to put a race down to feel good about myself. He helped me to see that my feelings of inferiority cause me to put people down. Instead of seeing myself as poor, black, and nothing, I began to understand who I was. I began to see my background, my history and my experiences as important.

The next conference I attended was a Tom Skinner conference. Tom was an articulate speaker who clearly spoke on racism. When he talked about racism, he hit both sides of the issue. He challenged me to be a part of the solution and not the problem. I began to see that I didn't have to be resentful. I realized that I was trying to be "too black."

I took some time to reflect back over my life. I had always had experiences with whites in one way or another. I was finally able to see this as God's plan and preparation. It was a part of my call to help bring reconciliation between the races.

Anytime we tease or ridicule a person about an unchangeable feature, or we resent our own unchangeable features, we are guilty of mockery. God promises to bring the mocker to "shame and confusion."

Ruthless witnesses come forward; they question me on things I know nothing about. They repay me evil for good and leave my soul forlorn. Yet when they were ill, I put on sackcloth and humbled myself with fasting. When my prayers returned to me unanswered, I went about mourning as though for my friend or brother. I bowed my head in grief as though weeping for my mother. But when I stumbled, they gathered in glee; attackers gathered against me when I was unaware. They slandered me without ceasing. Like the ungodly they maliciously mocked ; they gnashed their teeth at me.

O Lord, how long will you look on? Rescue my life from their ravages, my precious life from these lions. I will give you thanks in the great assembly; among throngs of people I will praise you.

Let not those gloat over me who are my enemies without cause; let not those who hate me without reason maliciously wink the eye.

They do not speak peaceably, but devise false accusations against those who live quietly in the land.

They gape at me and say, "Aha! Aha! With our own eyes we have seen it!" O LORD, you have seen this; be not silent. Do not be far from me, O Lord. Awake, and rise to my defense! Contend for me, my God and Lord. Vindicate me in your righteousness, O LORD my God; do not let them gloat over me. Do not let them think, "Aha, just what we wanted!" or say, "We have swallowed him up." May all who gloat over my distress be put to shame and confusion; may all who exalt themselves over me be clothed with shame and disgrace.

May those who delight in my vindication shout for joy and gladness; may they always say, "The LORD be exalted, who delights in the well-being of his servant." My tongue will speak of your righteousness and of your praises all day long. - Psalm 35:11-28

I had to learn to accept the "unchangeables" that combined to make me who I was, and who I am. I saw myself in the hands of the Potter and began to thank God for each aspect of my background and personality.

You too can cooperate with God in developing the Christ-like character in you. Begin to mediate on and memorize Scriptures that describe your identity in Christ. Here are some that helped me.

I no longer call you servants, because a servant does not know his master's business. Instead, I have called you friends, for everything that I learned from my Father I have made known to you. You did not choose me, but I chose you and appointed you to go and bear fruit — fruit that will last. Then the Father will give you whatever you ask in my name. - John 15:15-16

Now if we are children, then we are heirs — heirs of God and co-heirs with Christ, if indeed we share in his sufferings in order that we may also share in his glory. - Romans 8:17

Therefore, if anyone is in Christ, he is a new creation; the old has gone, the new has come! - 2 Corinthians 5:17

So I tell you this, and insist on it in the Lord, that you must no longer live as the Gentiles do, in the futility of their thinking. - Ephesians 4:17

For a more comprehensive list read "The Bondage Breaker," by Neil Anderson.

To bust down the walls of self-rejection, with God's help, I learned to accept the following ten things that I could not change. In accepting these things I began to get insight into just who I am in Christ.

PARENTAGE

I had to learn to accept my parents, their chosen vocations, their physical appearance, and any defects they had. This includes speech problems, physical or mental disabilities, and levels of intelligence. In addition, I must accept all the factors, circumstances and consequences in regard to my birth and childhood. Even loss of one or both parents would have been part of God's special purpose for me. I was able to begin to forgive my father for not being there when I wanted him to be. This was extremely significant because once I began to do this, I was able to see my father for the man God made him. My father was a pastor. A pastor is God's representative here on Earth who is to lead, protect, and tend His flock. This is not an easy task at all.

One of the ways that God helped me to grow in this knowledge was by giving me a church to pastor. The first time that I didn't make it to one of my own son's events, this point was driven home to me. So, I have come to learn that God has a reason for giving us the parents that we have. We may not be able to understand the reason why, but we must trust that God knows exactly what He is doing.

I will praise you, for I am fearfully and wonderfully made; Marvelous are Your works, And that my soul knows very well. My frame was not hidden from You, When I was made in secret, And skillfully wrought in the lowest parts of the earth. Your eyes saw my substance, being yet unformed. And in Your book they all were written, The days fashioned for me, When as yet there were none of them.
- Psalm 139:14-16 (NKJV)

RACIAL BACKGROUND

I also had to accept my racial heritage. This entails the historical consequences of circumstances and issues that my race has inflicted on others, as well as things that have been inflicted upon my race, strictly because of our racial identity. For African Americans, slavery is an example of the latter of these two issues. Christians in America, black and white, do each other—and ultimately God—a disservice by not dealing with this situation head on.

I don't embrace slavery—especially the American version. No Christian should embrace or make excuses for it. I realize it as a tragic part of the American landscape for more than 200 years. It is something that continues to affect our country and culture even in this century. I don't like the way my ancestors were treated. However, I don't desire to be anyone other than an African American, despite our history of slavery. I love myself, my heritage and the color of my skin that God has given me.

I am black but lovely, daughters of Jerusalem, Like the tents of Kedar, Like the pavilions of Salmah. Take no notice of my swarthiness, It is the sun that has burned me. - Song of Songs 1:5-6a (NJB)

NATIONAL HERITAGE

I accept my American heritage. This one can be a rough one for Americans, no matter your racial or ethnic background. America is commonly referred to as a "melting pot" (a misnomer that I will get to in the next chapter). Different people have come here from all over the world for different reasons—some genuine, others dubious. Many of us at some point or another in the brief history of this country have been at odds with our nation and the way it has treated either our ancestors or us. This is our country however, and we need to understand and accept our national heritage.

For you are a people holy to the LORD your God. The LORD your God has chosen you out of all the peoples on the face of the earth to be his people, his treasured possession. - Deuteronomy 7:6

TIME IN HISTORY

I was born at precisely the right time. God destined my accomplishments and failures. There was a reason that I was born and raised in the mid-20th century in America, and I have the challenge and the obligation to learn from past generations and leave a legacy of faithfulness for the future generations.

As Mordecai told Esther: For if you remain silent at this time, relief and deliverance for the Jews will arise from another place, but you and your father's family will perish. And who knows but that you have come to your royal position for such a time as this?" -

Esther 4:14

GENDER
I am very happy to tell you that I like the fact that God made me male. If you are female, you should be pleased that God made you female. We must however understand that with our genders come responsibilities that we must live up to.

So God created man in his own image, in the image of God he created him; male and female he created them. God blessed them and said to them, "Be fruitful and increase in number; - Genesis 1:27-28a

BIRTH ORDER
It was vital to understand the tendencies and unique characteristics of my birth order. This is something that many people do not pay enough attention to. God looks at the first born or first fruits as His. If I reject this benefit, it throws everything out of whack and out of sync. Look at the biblical examples of Cain and Abel and Esau and Jacob. I realize that as a first-born son I am particularly blessed. Eldest siblings in families are usually very driven. This is good to realize, since I know that I must balance my work habits in consideration of my wife and my health.

Jacob said to his father, "I am Esau your firstborn. I have done as you told me. Please sit up and eat some of my game so that you may give me your blessing." - Gen. 27:19

BROTHERS AND SISTERS
God ordained who my biological brothers and sisters would be and how many I would have. They played a crucial role in my character development, and will continue to impact my life. We do not pick who our siblings are or how they will relate to us. They are the first people that we learn to relate to, and who they are helps us to begin to learn to love unconditionally.

All his brothers and sisters and everyone who had known him before came and ate with him in his house. They comforted and consoled him over all the trouble the LORD had brought upon him, and each one gave him a piece of silver and a gold ring. - Job 42:11

Say of your brothers, 'My people,' and of your sisters, 'My loved one' - Hosea 2:1

PHYSICAL FEATURES

If my teeth are crooked, I can go to the dentist and get them straightened. If I break my nose, I can go to a plastic surgeon and get a nose job. My looks will change as I grow older. I will put on weight and lose weight, but who is it that God and ultimately people will see when they look at Haman? It is the inner man, or to quote Rev. Dr. Martin Luther King, Jr., the "content of my character" that people should see shining through. We must accept our physical features and develop inward character that is reflected in our outward appearance.

He grew up before him like a tender shoot, and like a root out of dry ground. He had no beauty or majesty to attract us to him, nothing in his appearance that we should desire him. - Isaiah 53:2

MENTAL ABILITIES

Since God created me with a specific purpose in mind, He has equipped me with the necessary skills, gifts and aptitude to accomplish His plan.

My son, if you accept my words and store up my commands within you, turning your ear to wisdom and applying your heart to understanding and if you call out for insight and cry aloud for understanding and if you look for it as for silver and search for it as for hidden treasure, then you will understand the fear of the LORD and find the knowledge of God. - Proverbs 2:1-5

AGING AND DEATH

We do not choose when we are born or when we die. As I grow older I am ever mindful that my time to fulfill God's purpose is limited. God has a purpose for me, and He has determined a time in which I am to fulfill that purpose. I must be cognizant of that and live my life accordingly.

Teach us to number our days aright, that we may gain a heart of wisdom. - Psalm 90:12

God's perspective is different from ours. He ordains every aspect of my identity and calls it good. When we fall into the trap of building walls of self-rejection, we are telling God that He has made some mistakes; that He is not omniscient. How can I question His sovereignty? To reject myself is to imply that God is not capable of designing His creation! The acceptance of these ten unchangeable things is the beginning of busting the walls of self-rejection and praising God for His goodness and His plan.

Yet, O LORD, you are our Father. We are the clay, you are the potter; we are all the work of your hand. - Isaiah 64:8

None of us needs to reject who, why, when, where and how God made us, or the experiences He has allowed us to go through in our lives. As we learn to accept God's plan for our lives, and as we accept ourselves, the walls of self-rejection crumble and fall. These walls cannot stand against love. As they fall, it becomes easier to see how God uses the varieties of color, personalities, backgrounds, cultures and experiences to make up a Body that will bring glory to Him. We will begin to long for the gifts that others have to pour into our lives.

Here's an example.

I am very much mechanically challenged. I couldn't tell you the difference between drywall or a wet wall; real wood or particle board. I don't do construction jobs! God has blessed me with a lot of gifts, but the gift of speaking in mechanical and construction tongues is not one of them. I also have no expertise when it comes to matters of heating and cooling a building. So whenever the furnace or the air conditioning unit at church is having problems, another member jumps in and saves the day. His name is Jim Henderson. He comes in with his toolbox and before you know it, the building is either warmer or cooler, depending upon what time of the year it is.

I'll say it right now: Haman Cross, Jr. loves him some heat in the winter and some air conditioning in the summer! I thank God that He blessed Jim Henderson with the special gifts and talents that he has, and I thank God that Jim Henderson is part of my flock. Jim Henderson is a Christian, a longtime member of our church, and Jim Henderson is white. Where would the Church be without him? It certainly wouldn't be as warm and toasty in the middle of January and February if we hadn't crossed colors!

Rosedale Park Baptist Church would not be the church that it is today without him. Jim keeps the heat on with his heating and cooling acumen, and I keep the heat on with God's Word. We play our vital roles and when we use the gifts and talents that God has given us to bless our church, we work as a well-oiled machine. There is a place for everyone in God's church: black or white, mechanically gifted or mechanically challenged!

Knowing, loving, and accepting myself allows me to function where God wants me to function—in His will.

Haman fit de' battle of self-rejection, self-rejection, self-rejection. Haman fit de' battle of self-rejection and de' walls came tumblin' down.

Oh, it is such a liberating feeling; working in your own gifts and loving the fact that this is the way that God made you! As the walls start to fall, we'll notice our loneliness in our walled-in existence. We'll allow cracks to form in our walls. We'll cut out some doors. We'll even tear down our walls to let in all God wants to give us through other people, especially those who are different. We'll acknowledge their mistakes. We'll confront as needed. We'll give to them those things that we are uniquely able to give.

Perhaps through my personal example, you can see why it's so vital to appreciate and love who you are and Whose you are. Understanding who I was and Whose I was became critically important for my growth and in the process of learning to love myself. I did it when I got kicked out of college, and for some reason I thought that would be enough—that would be all it took to knock down my walls. When God really began to bust the walls down in my life, He showed me that I still had some loving and appreciating of myself to do. If I didn't fully appreciate whom God had made me and why He put me here for such a time as this, I would never *Cross Colors*. And looking back on my life and ministries, I knew that crossing colors was one of the things that God had planned for me, long before I was born. I was born this way for a reason.

As the walls fell, I came to understand that one of the calls on my life was to do some wall bustin'. God wants me to help you bust some walls. For some it might be harder than others to do this, but keep in mind that this is something that God has commanded all of us.

I have preached at many rallies and conferences where the ideal of racial reconciliation has been taught. I have seen people of all races and colors cry and pray with each other as they have poured out their hearts in repentance and shame for how they have helped to build and strengthen the walls in all of our lives. Yet in America in 2014, I still needed to write this book, because I still know that the most segregated hour of the week in this country is Sunday at 11 a.m.

People of God, we have got to get serious! Oh, how we are grieving the heart of our God! So this is what I have begun to look for in people—as the United States Marine Corps says, "A Few Good Men." Really. I'm looking for the same thing that God has always looked for: A Few Godly Men! I won't sit here and be naïve enough to think that everyone who attends those rallies will leave there and do what they heard from the speakers, no matter how godly, biblical or true the sermon may have been.

Whether we want to believe it or not, there are people in the church you attend and even in the house that you live in that do not want to obey God— let alone attempt to *Cross Colors*. So let's just get real here—look into your own heart. Are YOU ready to *Cross Colors*? Look into the mirror and ask yourself that question, because if you are, you are one of the Few, the Blessed—the Chosen!

God has always spoken to the masses but chosen just a few to accomplish His goals.

But the Lord said to Gideon, "There are still too many men. Take them down to the water, and I will thin them out for you there. If I say, 'This one shall go with you,' he shall go; but if I say, 'This one shall not go with you,' he shall not go." So Gideon took the men down to the water. There the Lord told him, "Separate those who lap the water with their tongues as a dog laps from those who kneel down to drink." Three hundred of them drank from cupped hands, lapping like dogs. All the rest got down on their knees to drink. - Judges 7:4-6

Now while he was in Jerusalem at the Passover Festival, many people saw the signs he was performing and believed in his name. But Jesus would not entrust himself to them, for he knew all people. He did not need any testimony about mankind, for he knew what was in each person. - John 2:23-25

I'm looking for a few good and godly people, and so is God. No matter how passionately I express God's vision of having a church that lives with *koinonia*—one mind—there are going to be some people who are not going to listen to me. But they will listen to *you*. So take this seriously, because the world is watching us!

When the world looks at us, what do they see? They see that

having Jesus Christ in our lives means that our divorce rate is no different from that of the world; that partiality is still a major problem that we can't or won't face and defeat. If the world can't see that having Jesus Christ as our Lord and Savior makes any difference, what are we doing?

How many souls will we win for Christ with a message that tells the world that having Jesus Christ in our lives gives us no power and that our lives are no different from theirs? Why should a young African American make a decision for Christ if it means that other Christians are going to look at him and see a threat, and then treat him the way that the bigoted police officer is going to treat them?

Whatever happens, conduct yourselves in a manner worthy of the gospel of Christ. Then, whether I come and see you or only hear about you in my absence, I will know that you stand firm in one spirit, contending as one man for the faith of the gospel without being frightened in any way by those who oppose you. This is a sign to them that they will be destroyed, but that you will be saved—and that by God. For it has been granted to you on behalf of Christ not only to believe on him, but also to suffer for him. - Philippians 1:27-29

This isn't pleasing to God. And if it's not pleasing to God, let's just stop! We should all quit calling ourselves Christians, Children of the Light and all the other terms we use (or more appropriately, *misuse*), to let people know that supposedly we have a relationship with the God of the universe. Let's just stop playing church. Let's just stop pretending that we love each other. And let's definitely stop pretending as if we love God.

Let me make it real for you, because ultimately this is how it was made real for me. God knows my heart. Once I really began to face that fact, I had to realize that all my pretense meant absolutely nothing to God. Once I decided that pleasing God was more important than pleasing myself, I had no other choice but to *Cross Colors*. And have no doubt, there is still a huge problem among the people of God in this country. If we don't do something about it, we will face far worse trouble.

Jesus knew their thoughts and said to them: "Any kingdom divided against itself will be ruined, and a house divided against itself will fall. - Luke 11:17

9

❖

Stew Pot or Melting Pot?

"Dif'rent Strokes for Dif'rent Folks"
- Sly and the Family Stone
("Everyday People")

Whether you were born white or black is no mistake. Your color was determined by God's design. People say God is color-blind. Nonsense! The diversity He introduced into the human race was just like everything else that He does—an intentional and loving act. God has always known exactly what He was doing! It has been human beings who have turned race into an issue rife with division and contention.

Here in America, many Christians have taken the misguided idea of moving toward a lack of diversity to a new level.

We all live in a melting pot, isn't it wonderful?

NO! NO! NOOOOOOOOO!

If God had wanted us all to be melted into one uniform substance, don't you think He would have done that in the first place? God created diversity! Humans have decided that we will celebrate diversity in every aspect of this planet, except when it comes to us.

We listen to all types of music. We love to receive a bouquets made of different varieties of flowers. As children, we couldn't wait to open the box of Crayola crayons that had 64 colors and the little crayon sharpener on the back. We wanted all those colors so we could use them. Who still watches a black and white TV? Why do we want diversity everywhere except in our most personal relationships? This is a smack in the face of our Lord, a God who created diversity.

And God said, "Let the water teem with living creatures, and let birds fly above the earth across the expanse of the sky." So God created the great creatures of the sea and every living and moving thing with which the water teems, according to their kinds, and every winged bird according to its kind. And God saw that it was good.

God blessed them and said, "Be fruitful and increase in number and fill the water in the seas, and let the birds increase on the earth." And there was evening, and there was morning—the fifth day.

And God said, "Let the land produce living creatures according to their kinds: livestock, creatures that move along the ground, and wild animals, each according to its kind." And it was so. God made the wild animals according to their kinds, the livestock according to their kinds, and all the creatures that move along the ground according to their kinds. And God saw that it was good. - Genesis 1:20-25

It is most significant that God used a rainbow to seal His covenant with Noah. The rainbow, formed when light passes through water, is a simple enough equation that can produce all the colors needed to create every color imaginable. Light and water are two of the first elements that God created. This is a fact that I don't think should be lost on anyone.

Didn't God scatter the languages across the planet? Didn't He bring different races up across this planet?

Look at the many different colors and materials that God demanded be used when the Hebrews worshiped Him. I don't know about your god, but the God that I read about in Holy Scriptures is not a monochromatic God. He is a technicolor God!

This whole "melting pot" thing is something that ultimately separates us. One thing that burns me up is when I hear that tired old refrain from whites: "When I look at you, I don't see any color." If you don't see any color, what are you looking at? If you ever look at Pastor Haman Cross, Jr. and do not see a Christian who is African American, one of us needs to check ourselves.

I said earlier that we must change our syntax from calling ourselves African American Christians to Christians who are African American. But I did not say that we must eliminate that part of us. There is a very good and godly reason for this. God made me the way I am. If, in your attempt to explain to me that you are not into partiality, you tell me that you don't see a very significant part of me, you are in essence saying that you don't care about a very significant part of me. You are saying that who I am in Christ is not important to you, because Christ died for and lives in ALL of me, not just a part. In saying that, you are also telling God that His creation means nothing to you.

I praise you because I am fearfully and wonderfully made; your works are wonderful, I know that full well. - Psalm 139:14

Before I formed you in the womb I knew you... - Jeremiah 1:5a

Since God has given us all this diversity, this melting pot idea needs to be reconsidered by any Christian who wants to get past this whole partiality thing.

A melting pot is the way we've heard America described for a very long time.

That ideology is so prevalent that it's inscribed on all of our money; E Pluribus Unum—"From Many One."

Our American culture tells us that we all are thrown into a pot and melted down into one uniform product when it's all said and done, and that product is known as America.

Part of the thrust of American education has been to forget one's past (for those of you who struggle with black history) and become part of the new America, there continues to be a great pressure or heat to melt us into a uniform culture in America. Those in power have purposely attempted to keep the country from fragmenting into its many component parts. - Tom Hopler

What Mr. Hopler says is true. While on the surface this idea of a melting pot might seem quite admirable, it flies directly in the face of who we are and Whose we are. While God does call us all to be one, He is telling us to do it through Christ, not through some philosophy! God knew that diversity was going to bring about differences, so He spoke to this in His Word.

When you reap the harvest of your land, do not reap to the very edges of your file or gather the gleanings of your harvest. Leave them for the poor and the alien. I am the Lord your God. - Leviticus 23:22

If one of your countrymen becomes poor and is unable to support himself among you, help him as you would an alien or a temporary resident so he can continue to live among you. - Leviticus 25:35

These are Levitical laws, y'all! They were not some suggestion that God gave the children of Israel to do once they became liberal or enlightened. This was right up there with "Thou shalt not kill!"

Somehow, however, we've forgotten that here in America. We've forgotten that God made us all the way we are for very good reasons, because He is God and He does not make mistakes.

When we don't look at each other for the way God made us, we are saying: "Well God, this whole race issue is really all your fault. Why didn't you make us all the same?"

Whether we say it consciously or unconsciously through our actions, we should really check ourselves and put on some brakes. Remember the conversation between God and Adam in Genesis 3?

And He said, "Who told you that you were naked? Have you eaten from the tree that I commanded you not to eat from?" The man said, "The woman you put here with me—she gave me some fruit from the tree, and I ate it." - Genesis 3:11-12

Look at this scripture closely because there is a lot going on here: not only is Adam shifting the blame for this sin off of himself and onto Eve, but also he is shifting it all ultimately onto God! "The woman YOU put here with me…"

He's telling God that He made the mistake: *I was all right until you put her here—a little lonely, but all right.*

When we try to ignore our racial differences we are in essence telling God that He made a mistake. How dare we!

Because there are white people that I don't like, and black people that you don't like, and brown people that nobody likes, we try to clear up our sin by saying (and trying to sound noble while we say it): "God doesn't looketh at the color of thine skin."

I am black by design. It is not a mistake. You are white by design, he's yellow by design, she's brown by design, and they are red by design. All of us are designer originals, created by the Most High Designer. All the diversity that God has created is intentional. It is not a mistake! Once we realize that, we will be able to say, "It's all right to be white. I don't need to apologize for being Korean. God made me Latino and He always knows what He's doing!"

God has always made provisions for diversity. He's always provided for the minorities and the people on the fringes of life. And He has always expected His children to help them as well.

For the Lord your God is God of gods and Lord of lords, the great God, mighty and awesome, who shows no partiality and accepts no bribes. He defends the cause of the fatherless and the widow, and loves the alien, giving him food and clothing. And you are to love those who are aliens, for you yourselves were aliens in Egypt. - Deuteronomy 10:17-19

The melting pot is real, but it's not what we think it is. It is not a mixture of all people and all ideas. It is unbalanced and biased. Oh, it may start off with a little of this, a little of that, and a lot of this other thing, but if you think for one instant that it's going to remain that way you are crazy!

If I put a pound of tomatoes in a pot and throw in a dash of olive oil, nobody is going to come along after dinner and say: "Boy, Haman, that was some great tasting olive oil!" They're going to taste tomatoes, that's it! In a melting pot, the dominant culture actually takes over. And the further away from that dominant culture you are, the longer and harder it is going to be for you to melt—to assimilate.

If there are five of you and one of me and we decided that we needed to become a melting pot, whose is going to have to change the most? Who is going to feel the fire of that melting pot the longest? Me! How do you think that is going to feel? It's not going to feel good, and I don't want to feel like that any more than you do.

What we need to look at is the idea of a stew pot. In a well-made stew, you can see, feel and taste each individual ingredient that went into making the stew. There will be carrots, onions, peppers, potatoes and whatever kind of meat you want, and they will all combine to make up the stew! I know because my wife can make a great pot of stew. She might not put as many onions in the stew as she does potatoes, but you can still taste them, and you know that umm, there's some onions in there.

That's what the first-century Church looked like: Jews, Gentiles, males, females, rich and poor. The only image that they were all striving to become was the image of Christ. They all brought their histories, their experiences, their unique abilities to the church, yet they had *koinonia*—one mind. Not one color, not one sex, not one culture—one mind. That is why a stew is called a stew: it's a bunch of different individual things that have come together to make something else.

When you melt a bunch of things together, it's all uniform and you don't know what it is. Try it. Put some butter and sugar into a pot and melt it down. It's no longer butter or sugar; it's no longer a solid and you won't spread it on bread, or sprinkle it into a cup of tea.

The ideal of the Christian American church over the latter half of the 20th century was that of the melting pot. It should be plain to see that this idea will not work because we come from diverse cultures that should celebrate our diversity and not try to melt them into one homogeneous culture. The Church of America should have learned from that well-intentioned but misguided ideal that it is being changed into something else and has become an entity ripe for the rise of cults like the Mormons and the Nation of Islam.

We must love ourselves for who God made us. Our culture is part of who we are, and deciding to melt into some sort of a hybrid or sub-culture is not going to assist any of us with our growth or in learning to love ourselves and will retard the idea of love for others.

We—the Church of America—should go into the next millennium thinking about being a stew pot!

10

❖

Tough Talk

"If two people can't talk easily and comfortably but must forever guard against some slip of the tongue, some admission of what is in both persons' minds, they are likely to talk as little as possible."
- Margaret Mead
("The Egalitarian Error")

Good communication is essential in dealing with partiality and bigotry among the people of God. Did I say good communication? Scratch that. I mean great, fantastic, Holy Spirit-led communication! I cannot stress this enough! The communication has to be honest and open among us, which is the essence of true communication. In true communication there is sharing, learning and growth.

Then we will no longer be infants, tossed back and forth by the waves, and blown here and there by every wind of teaching and by the cunning and craftiness of men in their deceitful scheming. Instead, speaking the truth in love, we will in all things grow up into him who is the Head, that, Christ. From him the whole body, joined and held together by every supporting ligament, grows and builds *itself up in love, as each part does its work. - Ephesians 4:14-16*

The "body" metaphor that Paul uses in his letter to the Ephesians is important to the people of God's Church, particularly His Church in America. Many Christians wonder why the Church of America has been so ineffective and ridiculed. One of the major reasons involves the fact that we do not communicate. Wait. Yes, we do communicate things to each other all the time. However, the things that we communicate are separatism and individualism. We do not think of ourselves as part of one body!

We are a bunch of body parts walking around trying to do things by ourselves in our own time. We try to think without a Head. We attempt to run without legs; we want to touch without hands. We try to comfort, hold and hug without arms; and we ultimately try to fight a fight (a fight that has already been won for us, mind you) without fists!

All of this results from the lack of true loving communication among the children of God. The world sees this discrepancy even if we (Christians in America) don't see it. Our ability to advance God's Kingdom is directly impeded by our inability to live as we should. When the unsaved look at us, what do they see? Do they see people who are called to be in this world but not of it, or do they see people who just talk about being that way?

What does the Church of America really have to offer to the unsaved?

A divorce rate that is the same as the rest of the country...

A bunch of hypocrites who claim to love God, but worship idols...

A group of people that can work, drink and play together, yet sit in churches every Sunday knowing that the most segregated hour of the week is still 11:00 am Sunday morning...

The world knows this about us. They watch us talk outta' the sides of our necks! The world listens to us sing songs like, "Lord, I Want to Be a Christian," and then they see African American pastors give Louis Farrakhan a voice from their pulpits. The world watches as white churches move as far away from the inner city as they can get without completely leaving the planet.

The world listens as we sing, "Red and yellow, black and white we are precious in His sight. Jesus loves the little children of the world!" and "Oh How I Love Jesus," while we—American Christians—scream and spew pure hatred during the campaigns to desegregate the schools.

We cannot have or expect to spread true Christian love and values without true Christian communication—honest, "speak the truth in love" communication!

Just as with any love relationship (remember we're called to love each other), if there is no communication, the relationship is at best superficial. At its worst, it becomes a relationship of hatred and dysfunction, which is ultimately not worth anything at all.

True communication causes the participants to grow, which can be frightening, because we are once again moved out of our comfort zones.

I had many superficial relationships in my life because of walls (there's that word again!) that I erected to hinder good communication. I realized something about how sinister this whole partiality thing was when I was convicted about my communication or lack thereof.

First, I realized that I was just as guilty of partiality as the white Christians who I had been so angry with most of my life! I wasn't really communicating with them. I was just talking at them many times. Real communication requires listening with an ear of care and concern for someone. Isn't that what we expect of God when we speak to Him? How would we feel if after praying to God, He said, "Yeah, okay. Whatever. Next!"

This was how I was treating white Christians whenever they said something that I didn't like or agree with. Instead of really taking the time to discuss with them how that really made me feel, I would just blow them off as bigots, not even worthy of my time. That's partiality. That's destructive to God's people. It's telling someone that they are not important enough for me to really care about. Partiality is an equal opportunity sin—it doesn't discriminate.

The second major problem I discovered is that many of us have joined that partiality group and don't even know it. Partiality can exist in us unconsciously, so much so that I can think that I'm out doing the work of God and be ineffective and detrimental. Did I really think that when I was smiling in the faces of all those people that they couldn't feel my lack of caring and insincerity? I think sometimes black folks think that we can put something over on white folks. Here's what I thought. I could tell when there were all these phony white folks in my face, but there was no way that they could figure out that I was one of those phony black folk.

As I was convicted, I submitted to God. The true beauty of subduing myself and submitting to God throughout this process was watching the walls of distrust and anger being busted, while at the same time bridges of communication were being built.

Someone very wise once told me that there is nothing at all wrong with being ignorant. Being ignorant simply means that you don't know about something. Ignorance can be corrected and changed. We are all ignorant about things and that's how we learn. No one has to stay ignorant about things. But if you decide not to learn, not to broaden your mind, and to remain ignorant, then that's just being stupid. And there's a lot wrong with being stupid, which is basically defined in the Bible as being a fool. I have a big problem with that. And God has a huge problem with us being fools.

The fool says in his heart, "there is no God." - Psalms 53:1a

He who misgoverns his house inherits the wind, and the fool becomes slave to the wise. - Proverbs 11:29 (NJB)

A whip for the horse, a bridle for the donkey, and for the backs of fools, the stick. - Proverbs 26:3 (NJB)

As a dog returns to its vomit so a fool reverts to his folly. - Proverbs 26:11 (NJB)

Read those scriptures again! A fool has got nuthin' comin' from God!

So we must not be fools. This means that we must communicate with each other, and that communication must be open and honest. As we communicate with each other we will bust walls of ignorance concerning each other. When we build bridges through good communication, we may just find out that all black people can't dance; that we all aren't fast; that all white people are not stiff; that they all don't mistrust black people; and that we all have more in common than any of us ever thought possible.

Admitting to, recognizing and discussing issues that drive wedges between us are some of the first ways to begin open and honest communication.

Two issues that we face in this country that must be discussed openly and honestly are the issues of white privilege (yes it does exist), and black rage (yes it exists too). Pretending that one group makes more out of one issue than the other group, and acting as if this is something that we should all be able to get past is ignoring the issues and the chance to make head way in bustin' a wall.

White privilege has to do with the fact that, because of the society of partiality that we all live in, whites benefit because of the color of their skin whether they want to or not. It deals with the issue that the very fabric of our society gives them partiality and privilege, whether they want to receive it or not. This is an extremely touchy and difficult subject for many white Christians to deal with because of the fact that it takes admitting that many times not only have they benefited from this standard, but also that they knew and enjoyed benefiting from it.

Black rage is born out of anger and pain. Black Christians must admit that at some time or another in their lives, this rage has affected the way we perceive all whites in America. It is this black rage that will have Christian African Americans embracing the likes of Louis Farrakhan, not necessarily because of what he is saying but because of the color of his skin. Never mind that this man preaches and teaches a religion that is completely antithetical to Christianity. His color is what we relate to because of our rage at whites, Christian or not!

In 2002, I interviewed a group of Christians of varying ages, races and life experiences on these two issues. The following are some very open and honest stories of growth. Growth can be painful but sometimes if there is no pain, there certainly is no gain.

❖

Married Black Female, Age 30-40

I work as an engineer for a well-known company in the auto industry. In the department that I work in, you easily notice that the higher one moves up within the company, the whiter and more male it becomes. The people that you are going to be working with and for are white males. To say that I feel out of place would be a gross understatement. And I don't care how many times I read books about running with wolves and hear the lyrics, "I am woman hear me roar." Those things just don't make you feel any better about being surround by people that you just don't have a lot in common with. You just begin to realize and feel that you just really are not welcome there. It's just a kind of air or pressure that you feel when you go out to lunch or when you're sitting in a meeting. It's not overtly uncomfortable, but it's uncomfortable enough that you feel it. As an African American I just feel the pressure of working in a homogenized workforce.

I sometimes feel ashamed of how I felt that day, but I can't ignore or lie about it. I remember feeling so great when the O.J. Simpson Verdict came down. I was actually elated for a number of reasons. The first was because as an African American woman I knew in my bones that if his first wife had been the victim no one would have cared, no matter how much blood was spilled. Throughout the entire ordeal many black women understood that we (black women) would never be worth the ink or television time of a blond, blue-eyed white woman. That was an issue that was rarely ever talked about throughout all of the trial.

I didn't particularly like O.J. or feel really strongly about his innocence or guilt. I was just happy because he had gotten off. I remember looking at all of the faces of the white people when they heard the words: not guilty. I remember looking at the anger that all these white men were feeling and thinking, "now—maybe now—you have a small idea of how I felt when the cops who beat Rodney King got off." They were just so upset that I felt like laughing out loud at all of them. I didn't of course. But it still felt good.

If I had laughed out loud at all of them maybe then they could really feel how I feel when I read stories of black men being dragged behind cars, killed and then watch as they all laugh at the joke some jerk circulates about it throughout the office. Those jokes and pictures always end up in the hands of somebody black. It's just that many times rather than make a big fuss about it we just decide that it's pretty much what we're used to or thought would happen anyway. I guess that's why I felt so elated when the verdict came down, because finally there was something that I could really laugh about. In hindsight I know that the murder of two people and the suspect getting off is nothing to be happy about, but I still felt good. But even that good feeling was short lived, because I was still sitting there the next week when all their jokes about O.J. started circulating. I guess it would have felt better if I was sure that he hadn't done it, but it was like rooting for the bad guy in a movie. I just couldn't really get into it.

The shame of it all is that I couldn't believe how wounded all the white people were afterwards. A few of them came to me afterwards trying to get me to agree with them about how wrong the verdict was. It was actually pretty funny and sad to see them try to negotiate their way around that conversation without insulting me, because they seemed to want to say to me, "Don't you agree that the black jury is the reason he got off? Did they ignore the scientific evidence or did they not understand?" The whole situation seemed to make them a lot more uncomfortable than it made me. I still wonder why none of them ever tried to sit down and really talk to me about it.

I kept thinking of how many white juries had let white men walk away from murder charges when a black man had been lynched or killed. Nobody seemed to remember any of those instances. All they could talk about was how the judicial system had failed the families of those poor people. Where was all of this consternation when the LAPD was caught on tape beating a black man and still got off! Working in the white man's world is pretty difficult anyway; it makes it even harder when they leave no doubt in my mind that I, and my race, don't really mean anything to them as long as they get things the way they want them. We could have a hundred O.J. cases, and still not be even with them. It's like I'm keeping a tally of how many times they have gotten over on us, and they're up like a million to one, and they were upset about that one.

I have some white people that I would like to call friends, but it's hard to really trust them with my heart because I'm never really sure about them, or where they really are. And that hurts me. I know God doesn't like that whole attitude, but that's just where I am.

SINGLE WHITE FEMALE, AGE 25-35

This was a process, not a single event, and it is mixed with other things, so it is hard to describe.

Explaining how I came to understand white privilege is rather difficult because it is tied in with beginning to understand African American culture and seeing the nation's culture from a different perspective. It seems also, as I think about it, that there were a lot of small incidents or comments or attitudes over the years that had created an awareness in me that something like this exists. White privilege wasn't something that I thought about consciously or unconsciously growing up. When I first heard the term, I didn't know what to make of it. In hindsight I think about the times that it had been presented to me in such a way that I had tended to reject it, because of how it was presented to me and who was talking about it. Sometimes I thought that it seemed to make all white people out to be racists or bigots or something, and I never identified myself with that kind of a person.

However, just because I didn't identify myself with that kind of person didn't mean that I wasn't affected by the culture. I realized as I thought of this and as I have grown that there were some things and mindsets that I needed to change.

When I think about it, one of my high school teachers brought it up, not by saying there was such a thing as white privilege, but by pointing out inconsistencies and historical events. He told us about Thomas Jefferson having a black mistress, owning slaves, and yet writing that all men are created equal. He told us about the Berlin conference. He told us that the one black guy in our class wasn't really black black, but white black (this was how he put it for us), because he had grown up with us and had more of our white culture than his own black culture.

Some of these things I didn't understand because I didn't have a reference point, but in later years since, the things that he told us have begun to make more sense. He told us that Abraham Lincoln didn't just free the slaves out of good conscience but that it was a political move as well. That was shocking to me because I had learned about Abraham Lincoln the same way that every American school kid learns about him — that Abraham Lincoln was one of our greatest presidents because he freed the slaves, and that was it. I assumed like most people that he did it out of some high moral code only.

I guess, without actually saying it, this teacher had pointed out white privilege to us. Of course, he couldn't have come out and said that. Because really the things he told us were borderline controversial. This teacher was white.

I read a lot and in junior high and high school I read some books that affected how I looked at race relations. They were, "To Kill a Mockingbird," "Thorpe," and "Black Like Me." These books affected me because the main characters were white, but they identified with blacks by either helping them or posing as black. Because of this, they were attacked by the white society.

But, because all of these books were set in the South primarily and only one was a true story ("Black Like Me"), and they were all set either before I was born or before I had much memory of these kinds of things or situations, the effect that they had on me was somewhat nebulous. So even though my eyes were being opened to the fact that things like this happened, it wasn't real to me.

I had black friends and I guess I thought because I read those books and had a white teacher teach me some things about the discrepancies between races in this country, then I thought that I couldn't be affected by white privilege or bigotry. I was content with looking for it in other people and seeing other people's attitudes.

I was once in a ministry meeting when a comment was made about the way the ministry should be handled. All of us in the meeting were whites who were involved in inner-city missions. The person leading the meeting made it a point to drive home the idea to all of us there that no matter what, the "locals" did not need to know anything about the inner-workings of the ministry. It was all right to let them be involved in the ministry to a certain degree but there had to be limits as to what they needed to know or were privileged to. That comment was more than just words. It was expressing a mindset, a mindset that says it's okay to go help these poor people, of whatever race, but it's not okay to become friends with them, live with, live like them or accept them as equals. It actually felt very colonial, as if I was a missionary going away to some far off country and deciding that there was only so much that I was going to teach the "locals." The mindset seems to be that somehow accepting the minority culture as equal is perceived as rejecting the majority culture.

I know this because in college, my cousin was friends with some foreign students. I made a comment to my mom along the lines of what was wrong with my cousin that she couldn't find some friends of her own race. I didn't say it quite like that but that was the gist. In my mind, by getting so involved with foreign students, she was rejecting her own people or for some reason they rejected her. So even I had that attitude and mindset. Now people say the same thing about me and I see it from a different angle and I see that it was a prejudiced remark.

As I examined myself more, I continued to examine the American society and culture, and I noticed more and more that there were things that whites just didn't think about because we were never affected by it.

In college, I worked in a chain restaurant as a waitress. There were two black guys that worked there. One was the head cook and the other was a part-time cook/dishwasher. One day, one of the waitresses looked at the cook and said to him in a derogatory manner, "You all look alike." I don't remember any reason for her saying that. It seemed out of the blue to me. It made me see things differently because I didn't know that any of the workers looked at things that way. To me he was the cook and he was a good cook. He was black as a description of his appearance more than someone markedly different from me because of his skin color. After this incident, I heard the cook make comments about all of the black people working in the back and the whites working in the front of the restaurant. There was a black hostess for a while but I don't remember any other blacks working in the front. It was the first time I became aware that this kind of thing might actually exist despite civil rights laws, etc.

Another time that I realized that it is inside of our culture was when I watched "A Time to Kill" with a white friend, and she didn't get it. She didn't understand why the black guy was not convicted for shooting the men. No matter how much I tried, I couldn't explain it to her so she could understand it. The idea of the black man doing something like that and it being justified was too foreign a concept for her.

Once when I was in Florida, I went to visit a friend. At my friend's house we went to the beach. It was a very nice beach hidden near some beautiful homes, but it was a state or county park type of beach. A friend made the comment to me that it was probably a whites only beach. That never occurred to me because I am white and my friends were white and there was no sign and it was obviously a public beach. Anyway, I thought, "what if it was a whites only beach, even if there was no sign posted?" My next thought was that I'm white and I was allowed to take the advantages that come with it. At the same time, if I was with a black person and they wanted to go to the beach too, I would take them but I might warn them if I thought about it and knew the beach was like that. So I learned that everyone is affected by white privilege, whether they are black or white, prejudiced or not.

The next step in my life was being led to join a black church. By deciding to attend there I realized that much of my social life would be with black people and I would most likely meet black single men. The question came to my mind, "Was it racist to tell someone you couldn't date them because they were black?"

I hadn't really socialized with more than one black person at a time before, so this had never been an issue for me. I came to the conclusion that it was wrong to reject someone based on skin color despite the traditional reasoning behind it. The traditional reasoning was based on a racist line of thinking.

In researching this, I found that both blacks and whites were against interracial marriage and both had similar reasons. It was not just a white thing. This also made me see that I had these little prejudices that did not come out until there was a situation that brought them out. This was a revelation because I did not consider myself prejudiced. Through this, I realized that everyone has prejudices and that no matter how hard you try not to, you pick up things from your environment that prejudice you, sometimes subconsciously.

Through my socializing with these black people at my church I began to see that my theory of, "people are people" and "we're all Americans" was not true. It was true in the sense that people all want the basic things of love, trust, respect, etc. But how they showed it might be different. We are all Americans, but just as siblings growing up in the same family can have completely different views of the family, so different races can have different views of America.

I continued to grow and learn as best I could throughout all of this. A conference on racial reconciliation opened my eyes to something brand new. I didn't know we needed to be reconciled or why. As I began to explore this area and to hang out with other people who were learning about it too, what I began to see was that my friends in white America had no understanding or concept of racial reconciliation.

In the O.J. Simpson case, for the first time I was caught in the middle. I understood the white point of view but at same time I was beginning to understand the black view as well. My black friends told me the black side and my white friends told me the white side, and the views were very different. At a conference I attended, one of the white speakers spoke on racial reconciliation and I went up to ask him a question. Ahead of me was a black man and he said to the speaker something along the lines of, "In my heart I believe O.J. is guilty but it feels so good that he was acquitted." I was beginning to see how blacks viewed white privilege, but at the same time I had not really seen it for myself. When you are in the privileged group, you don't see things as privileges. They are rights. They are automatic.

Over my life, I've found that blacks in general are probably more friendly to whites than the reverse. I guess as the minority you almost have to be more open, but the friendliness is mostly surface. Just as in any true friendship, understanding the real person takes time and trust.

Seeing white privilege for myself requires me getting to know people who have been affected by it that are honest but that I can trust to not see things that do not exist. It also takes being with blacks in many situations so that you (whites) are at some point put in a situation that reveals the discrepancy. If a black person is with a white person in white society, that black person many times receives some validation because of their company, as if somehow being able to be with whites makes you alright. This occurs as well in the reverse, because now the whites are able to get some sort of validation that all this race stuff really doesn't matter. This makes it harder for the white person to see this concept of white privilege as well.

Along with these things, we have been told that people in the South are prejudiced but not people in the North. We know that this is a myth, but it is different when you actually see that it is a myth. I think because most of the real atrocities took place in the South, whites and blacks have this idea that we here in the North don't have to deal with certain issues, but that's not true. It is just a little more subtle, I think.

There are two incidents that stand out in my mind where I actually felt the rejection of two of my black friends by whites. The first is when I took one of my friends to some suburban bicycle shops looking for used bikes. In a couple of the shops I could feel that they felt very out of place and that the sales clerk also felt very uncomfortable. I couldn't decide if it was a racial issue or an economic issue. The second time, a friend and I went shopping in an outlying suburb and I really felt store owners watching us in many of the stores. I thought it was just me but when we got back to the car my friend brought it up and I knew it wasn't just me. This was my brave friend and she went back with me to this suburb because there was one store that had some gifts I wanted to buy. We couldn't find the store but we saw a building with a sign advertising some kind of gifts and decided to try that. We barely got in the door when a little old white lady ran after us asking us if we had some kind of registration tag. We could tell she was very uncomfortable with us and that it was because my friend was black. She told us that this show was for gift shop owners and not the general public. I still needed directions to the store I was looking for and decided to ignore this poor lady's hyperventilation and ask for directions. She gave us directions as she escorted us to the door. It was very enlightening for me because before, uncomfortable sales clerks have always managed to be polite and nice to me at least, but this woman was very obvious in her discomfort, to the point of being almost rude, although she tried to be polite.

Other things have come across in people's comments and questions to me. When my cousin came to visit a couple of years ago, he told me he heard Pastor Haman Cross, Jr. preach at a Promise Keepers rally in Kansas City. I asked him what he thought of it, and he said Pastor Cross preached on racial reconciliation and he couldn't relate to it. I thought about that and I thought about the fact that he probably has little to no contact with other races, and what contact he has had probably has not been enough to see any problems. Or they are like the kid in my class in high school, "white black," and that isn't how all black people are.

There are other things that have affected me as well but these are the highlights. I tried to be honest, so try not to be offended because I don't mean to offend. I really hope that this helps somebody, whatever race they might be, to get a little bit of understanding of how I discovered what white privilege meant to me.

SINGLE BLACK MALE, AGE 35-45
One of my earliest memories and visions of white people in

America came oddly enough the same way that I'm sure many whites in America have first encountered black people—via the TV.

I'm an African American born in the early sixties, and raised on TV. TV gave me some of my earliest memories and fantasies of life. TV took me to places I had never even heard of. TV let me live in the Florida Keys and own a dolphin as a pet; TV let me become a cowboy on any day of the week. I could even choose which cowboy I wanted to be on some nights. TV told me that with the right kind of detergent, my mother could make her whites whiter than white with eight essential vitamins was stronger than dirt, and had ten percent real fruit juice. TV was exciting, TV was loud, TV was necessary—or at least I felt it was. I watched it so much I thought it was an inalienable American right to spend hours watching the soft gray screen glow and move before my wide eyes (these were in the days of BLACK and WHITE, VHF only TV sets).

I thought of TV like a stove, a chair, the trees. In my mind, TV was just a part of the rest of the world—something that belonged.

As I think of it now, TV taught me at an early age how painful an addiction could be. The idea of going even eight hours without it sent my young mind and body into a panic. It was through that dominating box that I developed my first attitudes concerning whites, attitudes that would creep into my psyche' well into my 20's.

The visions of white-shirted men with crew cuts or soldiers armed with fire hoses, rifles or attack dogs were sobering. I had seen Moe, Larry and Curly bop each other with hammers, wrenches and two by fours for as long as I had been watching TV, so violence on that little gray shaded glowing screen was something that I had seen before—it was comical. The violence that I saw on the TV news was not comical however. It was real. The way the people moved; how they stumbled after being punched, kicked or swatted with a club did not resemble the way Napoleon Solo or Peter Gunn fell after a well-placed judo chop. The level of violence that was beamed into the den of my father's house in Detroit, MI from places with names like Selma, Birmingham, Meridian and Tuscaloosa was frightening. You could feel the hate coming off of the screen. The hate that was alive and well so far away from me was transmitted to me and was now tangible—I could feel it. As much as I loved sitting in front of that TV, as fond as I was of that magical box that took me to other places and into other people's lives, I found myself moving away from it whenever those images appeared. I found myself hiding behind my father's chair, peeking my head around it and watching the pictures or waiting until it was off before settling—however nervously—back down in front of it again.

I saw violence directed at people that looked like people that I knew— people who looked like my relatives here in Detroit. I saw white policemen surround a black man who looked like my Uncle Dave, and beat him to the ground with clubs. A man who resembled my best friend's father lay on the ground trying to cover his privates and face while another white man let the dog that he had on a leash rip at his legs, arms and anything else that it could bite.

Women! They were punching, shoving and turning hoses on women! Young black women, older Black women, it made no difference. Women who looked like Ms. Rosemary from down the street. These soldiers were knocking women down like they were grown men; turning fire hoses on them and knocking them over in the streets. That lady's dress flew up in the air and I can see her panties and bra... I can see her panties and bra on TV! I remember seeing a fat white man with a crew cut and beefy arms throw a young black woman to the ground and stand over her screaming at her.

This went against everything that I had ever learned in my few years on this earth. You didn't hit people with glasses and you never even considered hitting a female. The fire hoses went on though, knocking them all down, male or female. It didn't make any difference to that spray of water. It didn't make any difference to the dogs. It didn't make any difference to those white men. It was obvious that they didn't care. They hated those people who looked like me and my people.

One night I saw them interview a woman who looked like Mrs. Sharkey, one of my teachers! Cat-eyed glasses, grayed hair that was made up into a bun that rested on top of her head, and the thin lips that were decorated in what looked to be black lipstick since that was how our black and white TV represented the color red. The things that she said about "niggras" and how she didn't think they were like the rest of us humans made me sick. The next day at school I began looking at Mrs. Sharkey a little differently.

I was introduced to pure brutal hate when I looked into the faces of those white people on my parents' TV. I didn't know it then, but something had begun to sprout inside of me. I began to hate the white people that I saw on the news shows. Always questioning my father as to whether or not that was one of the mean white people or if they were a nice one.

I also had heard people talk about white people.

For the longest of times I thought of them as someone or something that I wanted to stay away from, even though it was clear from the context of the conversations that they walked amongst the rest of us—they even wielded a certain amount of power.

"Man, you betta' not let that cracker catch you doin' that."
"Honkies always got to be keepin' us down."
"Chile', I am sooo glad I don't have to look that peckerwood in the face no mo'…"

White folks—crackers, rednecks, peckerwoods, honkies—those were the terms I had heard adults use early on in my life. Inside I began to either fear and/or hate white people. They were not to be trusted. They hurt people who looked like me. This influenced me greatly as I grew up in a city that was and still is so polarized that many polls place it as the most segregated urban area in the country.

I grew up and thought I had become enlightened because I had dated a few white girls and had made some friendships with whites. But every now and then I would see something on the news, or read something in a magazine and all of those feelings of hatred would just rise right up to the surface, not slowly, but as if I had just watched those pictures from the sixties. I would get like that and go to work or out into public and just want to hurt white folks.

What ultimately helped me to change my view was making some very dear friendships with whites at jobs and in school. Finding out that we listen to a lot of the same music (jazz), and read the same types of books, and have the same sorts of interests (camping and fishing), made them real people to me. They were not just some "white folks/crackers/peckerwoods" who hurt and hate black people, but real friends. This took a lot of trust and time: a lot of really talking to them and getting to know them and allowing them to get to know me.

It has all helped to change a lot of attitudes I had and to diminish a lot of rage that started way back when I was young.

Robert Jensen Baltimore

Here's what white privilege sounds like:

I was sitting in my University of Texas office, talking to a very bright and very conservative white student about affirmative action in college admissions, which he opposes and I support.

The student says he wants a level playing field with no unearned advantages for anyone.

"Do you think that being white has advantages in the United States?" I asked him. "Have either of us," I asked, "ever benefited from being white in a world run mostly by white people? If so, could we call it white privilege?"

"Yes" he conceded. "There is something real and tangible we could call white privilege."

"So, if we live in a world of white privilege—unearned white privilege— how does that effect your notion of a level playing field?," I asked.

He paused for a moment and said, "That really doesn't matter."

I looked him squarely in the eyes and said, "That statement reveals the ultimate white privilege: the privilege to acknowledge that you have unearned privilege, but to ignore what it means and all of its consequences."

That exchange led me to rethink the way I talk about race and racism with students. It drove home the importance of confronting the dirty secret that we white people carry around with us every day: in a world of white privilege, some of what we have is unearned. I think much of both the fear and anger that comes up around discussions of affirmative action has its roots in that secret. So these days, my goal is to talk openly and honestly about white supremacy and white privilege.

White privilege, like any social phenomenon, is complex. In a white supremacist culture, all white people have privilege, whether or not they are overtly racist themselves. Simply by virtue of the color of their skin, they get unearned benefits. There are general patterns, but such privilege plays out differently depending on the context and other aspects of one's identity (in my case, being male gives me other kinds of privilege as well). Rather than try to tell others how white privilege has played out in their lives, I talk about how it has affected me.

I am as white as white gets in this country of ours. I am of northern European heritage and I was raised in North Dakota, one of the whitest states in the country. I grew up in a virtually all-white world surrounded by racism, both personal and institutional. Because I didn't live near a reservation, I didn't even have exposure to the state's only numerically significant non-white population, American Indians.

I have struggled to resist that racist training and the racism of my culture. I like to think I have changed, even though I routinely trip over the lingering effects of that internalized racism and the institutional racism around me. But no matter how much I "fix" myself, one thing never changes—I walk through the world with white skin, and therefore white privilege.

What does that mean? Perhaps most importantly, when I seek admission to a university, apply for a job, or hunt for an apartment, I don't look threatening. Almost all of the people evaluating me look like me—they are white. They see in me a reflection of themselves—and in a racist society, that is an advantage. I smile. I am white. I am one of them. I am not dangerous. Even when I voice critical opinions, I am cut some slack. After all, I'm white. My flaws also are more easily forgiven because I am white. Some complain that affirmative action has meant the university is saddled with mediocre minority professors. I have no doubt there are minority faculty who are mediocre, though I don't know very many. As Henry Louis Gates, Jr. once pointed out, if affirmative action policies were in place for the next hundred years, it's possible that at the end of that time the university could have as many mediocre minority professors as it has mediocre white professors. That isn't meant as an insult to anyone, but it's a simple observation that white privilege has meant that scores of second-rate white professors have slid through the system because their flaws were overlooked out of solidarity based on race, as well as on gender, class and ideology.

Some people resist the assertions that the United States is still a bitterly racist society and that the racism has real effects on real people. But white folks have long cut other white folks a break. I know, because I am one of them. I am not a genius. As I like to say, I'm not the sharpest knife in the drawer. I have been teaching full time for six years and I've published a reasonable amount of scholarship. Some of it is the unexceptional stuff one churns out to get tenure, and some of it, I would argue, is worth reading. I worked hard, and I like to think that I'm a fairly decent teacher. Every once in a while, I leave my office at the end of the day feeling like I really accomplished something. When I cash my paycheck, I don't feel guilty. But, with all that said, I know I did not get where I am by merit alone. I benefited from among other things, white privilege. That doesn't mean that I don't deserve my job or that if I weren't white I would never have gotten the job. It means simply that all through my live, I have soaked up benefits for being white.

All my life, white people have hired me for jobs. I was accepted for graduate school by white people. And I was hired for a teaching position by the predominantly white University of Texas, headed by a white president, in a college headed by a white dean and in a department with a white chairman that at the time had one non-white tenured professor. I have worked hard to get where I am, and I work hard to stay there. But to feel good about my work and myself I do not have to believe that "merit" as defined by white people in a white country alone got me here. I can acknowledge that in addition to all that hard work, I got a significant boost from white privilege.

At one time in my life, I would not have been able to say that, because I needed to believe that my success in life was due solely to my individual talent and effort. I was myself the heroic American, the rugged individualist. I was so deeply seduced by the culture's mythology that I couldn't see the fear that was binding me to those myths.

Like many white Americans, I was living with the fear that maybe I didn't really deserve my success; that maybe luck and privilege had more to do with it than brains and hard work. I was afraid I wasn't heroic or rugged; that I wasn't special.

I let go of some of that fear when I realized that, indeed, I wasn't special, but that I was still me. What I do well, I still can take pride in, even when I know that the rules under which I work are stacked to my benefit. Until we let go of the fiction that people have complete control over their fate—that we can will ourselves to be anything we choose—then we will live with that fear.

White privilege is not something I get to decide whether I want to keep. Every time I walk into a store at the same time as a black man and the security guard follows him and leaves me alone to shop, I am benefiting from white privilege. I do not like the fact that white privilege plays out in our daily lives, but it is clear that I will carry this privilege with me until the day white supremacy is erased from this society.

❖

These are just some examples of what partiality does to and in the body of Christ, and the rest of this country. However, we see that victory is within our grasp if we do the work to communicate and learn about each other. As Christians, we must first begin that journey by dying to ourselves and letting God have His way with us. Once we do that, our communication with Him will be better and so too will our communication with each other. Once we are able to do that, we are able to be involved in miracles.

11

❖

Partiality and Evangelism Make Strange Bedfellows

"I have a dream that one day the state of Alabama, whose governor's lips are presently dripping with the words of interposition and nullification, will be transformed into a situation where little black boys and black girls will be able to join hands with little white boys and white girls and walk together as sisters and brothers."
- Rev. Dr. Martin Luther King, Jr.
("I Have a Dream" speech, March on Washington, Washington, DC, August 1963)

"Only when Christ comes again will little white children of Alabama walk hand in hand with little black children."
- Billy Graham
1963

We've defined the problem as partiality. 1. Not total; incomplete. 2. Biased; prejudiced.

That's what the dictionary says, but in this chapter, let's get real.

Let's look at what has gone on in this country from its beginnings. Let's look at why we must still organize rallies and conventions about this issue, yet still not see any improvement.

Please indulge me and imagine—really imagine—yourself as me for a moment.

I'm African American, which is how I am classified in this country, so the roots of my family stretch back to the continent of Africa. My ancestors were brought here by and because of the slave trade in the United States. I'd like to share with you how I saw the African slave trade.

Slave traders at first bought slaves, but like all good capitalists, they came up with a system to spend less and sell the slaves for more. Kidnapping was one way, but then they discovered that they could go into a village, capture or kill a few of the men and they could enslave an entire community of people all at once! Men, women, children—it made no difference because their main concern was with being able to ship as much of their cargo as possible. There was a huge demand for free labor in the New World, and this was a way to provide it. And after all to them, these weren't really people anyway. They were just soulless savages.

Destroying families and whole communities of these beasts meant nothing—no harm done. In Africa and once they got here (if they survived the transatlantic death cruise), husbands were routinely taken away from wives; children were stolen from parents; babies were literally snatched out of the arms of mothers and sold to the highest bidder—never to be seen or heard from again. NEVER!

Imagine waiting in anticipation as your spouse spends nine months to deliver your child, and when the child is old enough to eat solid food (and sometimes before that) the baby is taken from you, and you never see that child again. This didn't just happen once.

Because my ancestors were thought of as chattel, "breeding" was encouraged so that more "cubs" or "pups" could be sold for profit. People have said that there is nothing more painful than the loss (death) of a child. I would submit to you today that there is nothing more painful than the loss (the taking away) of *children*, whom you'll never see again!

These people—my great-grandparents, my relatives—were forced to work in the industries that built this country. They worked from sun up to sun down; they were fed the least amount of food possible in order to keep them just alive enough to work (capitalism at work again). The men were routinely beaten and lynched, and the women were raped. These were my relatives who suffered this abuse, and it was my family that suffered it many times at the hands of the architects of America, the fathers of our country, whites in America... Christians in America.

As I wrote that last sentence, it occurred to me that maybe I should use quotation marks around the word, *Christians*. By doing that it would have signified that in my mind I question whether or not they were real Christians.

Did they read the same Bible as I? Did they pray to the same God?

How could a real Christian do or think these things?

If I had used quotation marks it would have made all of us (Christians) feel much better, wouldn't it? We could have read that sentence with quite a bit of pompous conviction, safe in the knowledge that who we are in Christ is as different from them as black & white. But I didn't use those quotation marks, because as far as I'm concerned and as far as I know, they were Christians! We all sin and we all fall short. And I can't say with conviction that we Christians have done much more for the reconciliation of our races than the world has.

We have gone from a country that didn't recognize a race of people as human, let alone capable of having a soul, to where we are today. And where is that?

I have had discussions with many white friends who cannot understand why some African American pastors seem to preach hate and separation to their congregations.

"What exactly are they saying?," I asked them.

"Well, they're giving people like Louis Farrakhan opportunities to speak from their pulpits," they reply.

"Do you know why they would possibly allow that?"

"No."

"They're preaching to hurt people. They are preaching to folks who feel like they'd rather have a Black Muslim speak to them than a white Christian. They also have been hurt themselves, often by white Christians who have professed to be their brothers and sisters in Christ."

Now before you close this book, think about that for a moment.

Come now, let us reason together...

Suppose your ancestors had been brought here against their will, as chattel to be worked to death. What if you had seen your husbands lynched, wives raped, children killed when your church was bombed? What if...?

I am not validating, encouraging, or supporting African American—or any— pastors who seem to mix and match religion with the politics of hate and partiality. But I must get you to begin to understand where I'm coming from if we are to go where God wants us to go.

The evangelical Church in America must face the fact that the way many Christians have represented God in the four hundred or so years here in the New World is nothing that would preclude Black folk—or any other non-whites—to want to have anything to do with "white Christianity," let alone be "evangelized" or "discipled" by one of them.

Malcolm X has been lionized through his martyrdom within the black community. He is especially attractive to many young African American males. You know what a young African American male is, right? They're the people that are always showing up at the top of the graphs, findings and studies that show up on the six o'clock news across this country. Studies that say things like:

Highest unemployment rate...
Highest number of high school drop-outs...
Highest percent of criminal convictions...
Highest number murdered...
Highest...

You see where I'm going.

These are the fathers of our children and the husbands of our daughters and we are losing them to the enemy because we are choosing a lie over the truth, society's numbers over God's Word, and fear over faith. We are not trying to address the needs of this group of God's people or understand them and where they live, or where they can go. Because of the disenfranchisement that these young men experience, they fall back onto something that gives them some sort of esteem, and this leads them toward Malcolm X. I'll discuss him in more detail later, but we need to acknowledge him in the context of what he presents to the African American community, and young African American Males in particular.

"The Autobiography of Malcolm X" is on the reading list of many inner-city public school systems' English and literature classes. This means that this book is going to be read by everyone in those classes, Christian or Muslim, saved or unsaved. Just as many people can recall and were influenced by the works of Shakespeare, Poe and Twain from having read them in their high school English class, now "The Autobiography of Malcolm X" is influencing many African Americans.

If you have never read it, here is an excerpt from chapter one:

When my mother was pregnant with me, she told me later, a party of hooded Ku Klux Klan riders galloped up to our home in Omaha, Nebraska, one night. Surrounding the house, brandishing their shotguns and rifles, they shouted for my father to come out. My mother went to the front door and opened it. Standing where they could see her pregnant condition, she told them that she was alone with her three small children, and that my father was away, preaching, in Milwaukee. The Klansmen shouted threats and warnings at her that we had better get out of town because "the good Christian white people" were not going to stand for my father's "spreading trouble" among the "good" Negroes of Omaha with the "back to Africa" preachings of Marcus Garvey.

My father, the Reverend Earl Little, was a Baptist minister...

Read it over again, and then read it a third time as an African American might. Does it affect you the same way when you read it as someone who is prone to distrust whites to begin with? Please, whatever you do, do not look at this as the rantings and ravings of someone who was prejudiced himself, because that fact pales in comparison to the history of this country. This is an extremely powerful paragraph to read, especially given the history of the Church in this country. Here you have a pregnant mother being threatened by the Klan, who represent "the good Christian white people," telling her and her husband who is a Baptist minister to get out of town. Please, whatever you do, pay attention to that scene, because it is fact, not fiction. Christians can no longer afford to not understand what that means for all of us. That is one of the reasons you see and hear some of the things that you do from African American pastors and their churches, and we cannot continue to ignore, disclaim, or discredit it. Because Malcolm X's family wasn't the only family this happened to.

Most Christians in America historically could have cared less about blacks. For the longest time they viewed us as being inhuman. Since we weren't human that meant that we didn't have souls, so why should they care if we went to heaven or hell? We were property. A slave owner would no more think of giving the Gospel to a slave as he would to one of the chickens in his yard!

This began to change during the 1700's as some whites began advocating the spread of the Gospel among the Negroes. From all of this sprang up the beginnings of an evangelical revolution within this country that led to whites and blacks worshipping together, albeit on separate pews. As more and more white Christians began to question the ethics of slavery, many southern whites began using the Bible to defend slavery in an attempt to stop the tide of abolition.

Here is a list of some of the reasons that the southern church leadership gave in support of slavery:

BIBLICAL REASONS
- Abraham, the "father of faith," and all the patriarchs held slaves without God's disapproval (Gen. 21:9-10).
- Canaan, Ham's son, was made a slave to his brothers (Gen. 9:24-27).
- The Ten Commandments mention slavery twice, showing God's implicit acceptance of it (Ex. 20:10,17).
- Slavery was widespread throughout the Roman world, and yet Jesus never spoke against it.
- The apostle Paul specifically commanded slaves to obey their masters (Eph. 6:5-8).
- Paul returned a runaway slave, Philemon, to his master (Philemon 12).

Charitable and Evangelistic Reasons
- Slavery removes people from a culture that "worshipped the devil, practiced witchcraft and sorcery" and other evils.
- Slavery brings heathens to a Christian land where they can hear the Gospel. Christian masters provide religious instruction for their slaves.
- Under slavery, people are treated with kindness, as many northern visitors can attest.
- It is in the slaveholders' own interest to treat their slaves well.

Social Reasons
- Just as women are called to play a subordinate role (Eph. 5:22; 1 Tim 2:11-15), so slaves are stationed by God in their place.
- Slavery is God's means of protecting and providing for an inferior race (suffering the "curse of Ham" in Gen. 9:25 or even the punishment of Cain in Gen. 4:12).
- Abolition would lead to slave uprisings, bloodshed, and anarchy. Consider the mob's "rule of terror" during the French Revolution.

Political Reasons
- Christians are to obey civil authorities, and those authorities permit and protect slavery.
- The Church should concentrate on spiritual matters, not political ones.
- Those who support abolition are, in James H. Thornwell's words, "atheists, socialists, communists [and] red republicans."

Throughout history people, who couldn't spell "love" if you spotted them the "l" and the "o," have used the Bible to justify their ends, and this list shows no difference. However, I have reprinted it here for a number of reasons.

First, to give you an idea of the mind frame of 19th century southern Christians (and many blacks would tell you that that view hasn't really changed in some states). Second, while this type of information may not pop up in many white churches in this country, it is distributed not only among black Christians, but within the entire black community, and is often used as ammunition by groups like the Nation of Islam to lead black folks away from Christianity. If people being led astray and away from Christ doesn't bother you, then you shouldn't be reading this book, and you definitely need not pick up the Bible and call yourself a "Christian" (note quotation marks).

A good tree cannot bear bad fruit, and a bad tree cannot bear good fruit. Every tree that does not bear good fruit is cut down and thrown into the fire. Thus, by their fruit you will recognize them. Not everyone who says to me, 'Lord, Lord,' will enter the kingdom of heaven, but only he who does the will of my Father who is in heaven. Many will say to me on that day, 'Lord, Lord, did we not prophesy in your name, and in your name drive out demons and perform many miracles?' Then I will tell them plainly, 'I never knew you. Away from me, you evildoers!' - Matthew 7:18-23

But all of this is history, right? Haven't we all come further than that? We have come further, yet we need to do just a bit of critical thinking here. While previously partiality was overt and accepted in the church, we have become much more subtle at our levels of partiality. It is now being practiced covertly, because the Church no longer accepts it—at least outwardly.

Before the Emancipation Proclamation was signed, in the 18th and 19th centuries, blacks and whites worshiped together, albeit on different pews. Here we are, moving into a new millennium and now we've advanced to the point that we are worshipping not in the same church on different pews, but in different churches altogether. So the question that begs to be answered is, "what's up?"

Here are some findings.

"Residential integration and segregation studies continually show that the degree of segregation between blacks and non-blacks is far greater than between any other two racial groups in the United States. Further, outside the South, the greater the percentage of African Americans in an area, the greater the level of segregation. In other words, because most other Americans prefer limited contact with African Americans, increasingly higher levels of segregation are needed as the proportion of African Americans increases. Segregation is not merely separation but, in the contemporary United States, is hierarchical. Residential segregation by race, researchers show us, isolates African Americans, and concentrates poverty and social problems in their neighborhoods." ("Divided By Faith", Emerson/Smith)

What does this mean? This means that while we are all sitting at reconciliation rallies, and locking arms and singing "We shall overcome" on Rev. Dr. Martin Luther King, Jr.'s birthday, when we leave these places we go back to the status quo. Not only do we go back, but this is also the way the majority of white Americans want it. These are the facts that African Americans intrinsically know and feel and many times cannot adequately articulate to the rest of the country. And it is this feeling of being undesirable; of being sold into the slavery of the white man's Jesus, that gives many of us a real sense of hopelessness. No Christian should feel this way about other Christians. Ultimately, it is that sense of hopelessness that we see erupt and boil over into riots in the streets of St. Louis, Los Angeles, Miami, Cincinnati, and who knows where next!

These are the cold hard facts of a cold hard lesson. What are we going to do about it?

What do we do when it seems that the people whom we are to call brothers just either don't want to be our brothers, or in their attempts to share their Gospel with us, continue to isolate and demean us even more?

I have a very dear friend who is now back in fellowship, but had left the church completely because of the hypocrisy and partiality that he both saw and experienced in the church. This wasn't someone who was drawn away from the church by Malcolm X and the Nation of Islam rhetoric; this was a saved believer that was chased away by Christians (no quotation marks)! That grieves God's heart!

Can we for a moment try to truly empathize with Rev. Dr. Martin Luther King, Jr.? Dr. King was one of the most passionate and articulate orators concerning the partiality problem that this country has produced. One of the most powerful pieces of literature ever written about our partiality in this country was written by Dr. King as he sat in a jail cell in Birmingham, Alabama. Within that letter, he very eloquently explains why no one in this country had the luxury of waiting for the basic civil rights of people to be put into place.

He explains "Why We Can't Wait" to a group of clergymen. This letter was not written to politicians, newspapermen, or a group of "atheists, socialists, communists [and] red republicans." This letter was written as a response to a public statement given by eight "fellow clergymen from Alabama." These were other men of God who really didn't like the fact that basically Dr. King had decided that there was no more time for business as usual. In his letter, Dr. King introduced them to what life was like for African Americans in this country:

"Beyond this, I am in Birmingham (Alabama) because injustice is here. Just as the eighth century prophets left their little villages and carried their 'thus saith the Lord' far beyond the boundaries of their home town, and just as the Apostle Paul left his little village of Tarsus and carried the Gospel of Jesus Christ to practically every hamlet and city of the Greco-Roman world, I too, am compelled to carry the Gospel of freedom beyond my particular home town. Like Paul, I must constantly respond to the Macedonian call for aid.

...I guess it is easy for those who have never felt the stinging darts of segregation to say wait. But when you have seen vicious mobs lynch your mothers and fathers at will and drown your sisters and brother at whim; when you have seen hated filled policemen curse, kick, brutalize, and even kill your black brothers and sister with impunity; when you see the vast majority of your twenty million Negro brothers smothering in an air-tight cage of poverty in the midst of an affluent society; when you suddenly find your tongue twisted and your speech stammering as you seek to explain to your six-year-old daughter why she can't go to the public amusement park that has just been advertised on television, and see tears welling up in her little eyes when she is told that Funtown is closed to colored children, and see the depressing clouds of inferiority begin to form in her little mental sky, and see her begin to distort her little personality by unconsciously developing a bitterness toward white people; when you have to concoct an answer for a five-year-old son asking in agonizing pathos: 'Daddy, why do white people treat colored people so mean?;' when you take a cross country drive and find it necessary to sleep night after night in the uncomfortable corners of your automobile because no motel will accept you; when you are humiliated day in and day out by nagging signs reading 'white' men and 'colored:' when your first name becomes 'nigger' and your middle name becomes 'boy' (however old you are) and your last name becomes 'John,' and when your wife and mother are never given the respected title 'Mrs.;' when you are harried by day and haunted by night by the fact that you are a Negro, living constantly at tip-toe stance, never quite knowing what to expect next, and plagued with inner fears and outer resentments; when you are forever fighting a degenerating sense of 'nobodiness'—then you will understand why we find it difficult to wait. There comes a time when the cup of endurance runs over, and men are no longer willing to be plunged into an abyss of injustice where they experience the bleakness of corroding despair. I hope, sirs, you can understand our legitimate and unavoidable impatience."

Please before you go any further, reread that portion of the letter and try to imagine yourself writing it. Just for a moment, try to feel that hurt, that pain, that frustration and that despair. Please, in the name of Jesus, imagine this.

This letter was written in April of 1963. While some of the situations have changed, the feelings and the environment that produces those feelings are still very prevalent within the African American community. A very telling sentence, one that all African Americans can still identify with (if they will be honest with themselves), speaks of "when you are harried by day and haunted by night by the fact that you are a Negro, living constantly at tip-toe stance, never quite knowing what to expect next, and plagued with inner fears and outer resentments." This speaks to the fact that blacks feel the pressure of racial profiling.

We worry about being pulled over by law enforcement for the dubious DWB (Driving While Black) charge. Blacks were shocked and amazed, but not at watching the videotape of the Rodney King assault (and what seems like daily incidents of police brutality against black people since then); we were shocked that so many whites couldn't believe that it occurred. This is one of the major points of misunderstanding and miscommunication, or maybe more aptly non-understanding and non-communication between us.

Is the Church content to leave the gap between races alone or shall we bridge the gap? If we are to bridge that gap, it is going to take people that are unwilling to continue on the path that we have been traveling on, no matter what society tells us to do or how we should react.

The gap is there often times because many blacks feel that white Christians are more concerned with the status quo of this society than they are with doing what God would have us do, as the body of Christ. Will we continue to do the things that have gotten us to the place where we are currently or will we truly trust God and change?

"Because evangelicals view their primary task as evangelism and discipleship, they tend to avoid issues that hinder these activities. Thus, they are generally not counter-cultural. With some significant exceptions, they avoid "rocking the boat," and live within the confines of the larger culture. At times they have been able to call for and realize social change, but most typically their influence has been limited to alterations at the margins. So, despite having the subcultural tools to call for radical changes in race relations, they most consistently call for changes in persons that leave the dominant social structures, institutions, and culture intact. Evangelicals usually fail to challenge the system not just out of concern for evangelism, but also because they support the American system and enjoy its fruits. They share the Protestant work ethic, support laissez-faire economics, and sometimes fail to evaluate whether the social system is consistent with their Christianity." ("Divided By Faith," Emerson/Smith)

The following question could be posed to both black and white Christians in America: For whom all did Christ die for on the cross two thousand years ago? Do African American Christians, who try to synthesize their theology with Afrocentrism, ask this question of themselves? Do white American Christians, who try to ignore and forget the past and present society, ask this question of themselves?

It would appear that either the question is not being asked, or it is being asked and when the answer comes, it is conveniently misplaced or tabled somewhere behind our priorities. Or it could be that like many of the Jews of Jesus' day who believed that God was only their God, they believe that Christ died for only them and their kind.

For Christ's love compels us, because we are convinced that one died for all, and therefore all died. And he died for all, that those who live should no longer live for themselves but for him who died for them and was raised again. So from now on we regard no one from a worldly point of view. Though we once regarded Christ in this way, we do so no longer. Therefore, if anyone is in Christ, He is a new creation; the old has gone the new has come! All this is from God, who reconciled us to himself through Christ and gave us the ministry of reconciliation: that God was reconciling the world to himself in Christ...And he has committed to us the message of rec-

onciliation. We are therefore Christ's ambassadors, as though God were making his appeal through us. We implore you on Christ's behalf: be reconciled to God. - 2 Corinthians 5:14-20

WWJD?

In the 1990's, the letters were printed on everything from bracelets to bumper stickers. They were literally everywhere. I once asked a young woman on a college campus about her WWJD bracelet and the significance of it in her life.

"Oh, it doesn't really mean anything," she said. "You know, everybody's wearing them so I got one, and I really like the colors."

"You mean you don't know what the initials stand for?"

"No, not really. Aren't they like the name of the designer or something?"

WWJD. DKNY. FUBU. MTV.

We need to examine some things when Christ becomes a fashion statement, most importantly ourselves and our witness. We live in a moment in time when everything is minimized, shortened and trivialized so that it can fit into a ten-second sound byte. We need to be very careful that we don't minimize or trivialize the importance of our Lord and of the roles we are to play on this planet. Are we truly living our lives as the salt of the earth? Are we being in this world but not of it? Do we proudly display our relationship with God so that He knows we love Him? Or is it just a superficial fashion statement that has been synthesized to fit into our culture?

When trying to sympathize with each other, when we are attempting for just a moment to walk in our brother's shoes, are we seeing from our brother's POV (Point Of View)?

When you see the anger and resentment of African Americans, are you looking at it with fear and trembling, anger, or deciding that you just don't care? Or are you really trying to get into their shoes, no matter how tight and uncomfortable they are? Are you more comfortable with the idea that your salvation is secure and that if you stay away from those kinds of people, then you are all right? Trust in this: if my children suffer, so will yours. Evil is not content to stay in just my neighborhood. It wants to get out and destroy everything (John 10:10). We are all in this together.

Now the body is not made up of one part but of many. If the foot should say, "Because I am not a hand, I do not belong to the body," it would not for that reason cease to be part of the body.

And if the ear should say, "Because I am not an eye, I do not belong to the body," it would not for that reason cease to be part of the body. If the whole body were an eye, where would the sense of hearing be? If the whole body were an ear, where would the sense of smell be? But in fact God has arranged the parts in the body, every one of them, just as he wanted them to be. If they were all one part, where would the body be? As it is, there are many parts, but one body.

The eye cannot say to the hand, "I don't need you!" And the head cannot say to the feet, "I don't need you!" On the contrary, those parts of the body that seem to be weaker are indispensable, and the parts that we think are less honorable we treat with special honor. And the parts that are unpresentable are treated with special modesty, while our presentable parts need no special treatment. But God has combined the members of the body and has given greater honor to the parts that lacked it, so that there should be no division in the body, but that its parts should have equal concern for each other. If one part suffers, every part suffers with it; if one part is honored, every part rejoices with it. — 1 Corinthians 12:14-26

White Evangelicals, when you move toward reconciliation, are you moving forward with the attitude of meeting minorities where they are? This is WJWD (What Jesus Would Do). Or do you approach it from the standpoint of ICRTYPOV (I Can't Relate To Your Point Of View)?

Those of us who know what WWJD means should really incorporate this into our lives.

This is of major importance when we *Cross Colors*.
What Would Jesus Do?
When Christ spoke to the Samaritan woman at the well, He approached her from a position of not only love but with knowledge about who she was. Christ knew her intimately, and because of this He enabled her to see Him for who He was in spite of all the divides and issues that were at work in her life. Christ approached her, knowing her cultural history and significance as well as His own cultural history and significance. Christ knew of the divide between the Jews and the Samaritans and He knew of the feelings of superiority and inferiority that were common place between these two groups. Jews literally hated Samaritans and thought of them as

dogs. Look at what Scripture tells us about what the disciples—all Jews—did when they saw Jesus talking to the woman.

Just then his disciples returned and were surprised to find him talking with a woman. But no one asked, "What do you want?" or "Why are you talking with her?" - John 4:27

Although the scriptures tell us that none of them asked those questions, it's obvious that those questions were at the forefront of their minds because they were surprised to find their teacher speaking to her. They didn't voice their feelings of bigotry more than likely because of fear of rebuke from their Lord. However they still thought these things.

You'll notice that none of them spoke to or greeted her. The Jews of Christ's area and time would do anything to avoid Samaria or a Samaritan! It is common knowledge that Christ's disciples took Him everywhere but through Samaria on their journeys. They were so caught up in their partiality that they were even willing to delay the work of Jesus by taking the long way around Samaria at different times throughout His ministry. Think about that: letting your own issues of hate, anger and partiality slow down the work of the Lord! All of this because of the fact that in their culture, those Jews were not willing to identify or even attempt reconciliation with the Samaritans.

Look at the similarity between what was going on then and what's happening now. In first century Palestine, the disciples would take the long way around Samaria so that they wouldn't have to go through it, even though the shortest distance between two points is a straight line. In the Detroit metropolitan area, which is considered to be the most segregated city in the country, the suburbs expand and grow outward, with no thought of how this continues to affect everyone (the people in the city and out).

Just as the Jews would take longer trips on roads that would allow them to bypass Samaria, freeways are built throughout this country so that people can either bypass the inner city, or have the quickest entrance and exit from the cities if they happen to work there.

Samaritan women of that day went to the well twice a day; once in the morning and once at night. The woman was at the well at noon to avoid being seen by the community at large. How many people in this country are ashamed of who they are because of the way the larger community perceives them, and are consequently disenfranchised?

I have been in all white neighborhoods and been asked the question: "What do you want?" I've heard other whites, thinking they were out of ear shot saying to people who were talking to me or my children, "Why are you talking with them?"

Jesus had no reason to bring cultural, ethnic or racial differences up with the Samaritan woman because He was there to deliver her. What we should see from this passage of scripture is that Christ was the only One who was going to reach that woman because of His love for her and His acknowledgment of who she was. The Gospel is for everyone, not just people who look, act, talk and think like us.

Yes, she was from another race that was treated with very little respect. Yes, she obviously was rebelling against the status quo culture of the day by talking to a man in public. Yes, she had problems with infidelity, promiscuity and had a bad reputation. Yes, she was not one of the mainline people of Jesus' cultural day. She was on the fringes, wounded and hurt by her past and disillusioned by the prospect of her future, but Christ went to where she was and spoke to her. He evangelized this woman.

And look at what happened after she was shown who Christ was to her and the world!

Many of the Samaritans from that town believed in him because of the woman's testimony, "He told me everything I ever did." So when the Samaritans came to him, they urged him to stay with them, and he stayed two days. And because of his words many more became believers. - John 4:39-41

That's what happens when you share the Gospel. That's what happens when you go and meet people where they are, without fear or prejudice. That's what happens when you bust a wall. That's what happens when you Cross Colors. The power of Christ is made manifest. It is released to do that which it was meant to do!

We have to go where people are, though. We cannot and should not build walls blocking people's cultures and realities, no matter how foreign they may be to our own reality.

In 1995, Bill McCartney, founder and leader of Promise Keepers, twice addressed the annual meeting of the National Black Evangelical Association. He spoke on the theme of reconciliation and Promise Keepers' commitment to overcoming racial division. That commitment was questioned by some at the conference: "What is Promise Keepers going to say about the anti-affirmative action atmosphere in this country? What are the men in stadiums this summer going to hear about that?" McCartney did not directly answer the questions, and the questioners were less than satisfied.

So too are some other black—and a few white—evangelical reconciliation leaders. Tony Evans, a reconciliation leader and head of the Urban Alternative in Dallas, said in an interview with Christianity Today, "The concerns of black Americans are not of dominant concern, by and large, to white evangelicals." The article went on to claim that "Evans's opinion may sound extreme to many white Christians, but among black evangelicals, he is in the mainstream."

According to Tony Warner, Associate Regional Director for InterVarsity Christian Fellowship, "White evangelicals are more willing to pursue a white conservative political agenda than to be reconciled with their African-American brothers and sisters. It raises a fundamental question of their belief and commitment to the biblical gospel." ("Divided By Faith," Emerson/Smith)

As Christians, we must keep in mind that we are to be about advancing God's Kingdom and forwarding His agenda, not society's or our own. To really bust a wall and Cross Colors, God calls us to do things that we normally wouldn't do. We must be willing and able to go to the well and speak to a Samaritan woman with whom we have nothing in common either culturally or historically. We have to spread the Gospel of Jesus Christ and let people—all people— know that His love, just like His blood, covers all our sins.

This is a radical idea, but that is exactly what the Gospel of Jesus Christ was in the first century, a truly radical idea that made the status quo uncomfortable.

That's what evangelism was about in the early church.

12

❖

What We Believe (Really)

"Write about what you know."
- Kurt Vonnegut

Here's the situation: God loves us. He wants us to love one another. We don't have any more time to waste in not doing that. Christians in America, let's wake up and look at things. If we can set aside our problems to dig out of the rubble of the 9/11 disaster; if we can rebuild New Orleans after Katrina; if we can forget all of our petty differences and look at the bigger picture as it pertains to our country; why can't we bust down the wall of partiality for God? If you have not thought about crossing colors, make that your goal now.

Let me make it real for you. The main reason some of us have not busted the wall of partiality is because we either don't think hell is real or we think we can live in hell.

"What?," you ask. "What are you talking about Pastor Cross? Of course I know hell is real...don't I?"

We don't think hell is real, that's one of our biggest problems.

How can I say that?

Because if the truth be told, if we were asked to do the work to *Cross Colors*, many of us would be more concerned with:

Who we might offend or how we might be offended.

Who might begin coming to and even join our church.

Who might move in down the block from us.

Whether our child is dating or (*ohmyGod*) marrying someone of a different race.

That's what I'm talking about. Are our hearts, minds and souls more concerned about what the world says or are we more concerned with what God says and what He thinks of us?

Do we have more fear about letting someone from a different background than us into our lives or are we more scared about possibly not doing the will of God? It is time to tell the truth. Quit hiding behind our piety and our good works. Confess your sins and destroy the devil's power over this area in your life. I dealt with that, because I didn't want to go home to be with the Lord and have him say to me: "SORRY, BUT I SAW NO DIFFERENCE IN YOUR LIFE OR YOUR HEART EVEN THOUGH YOU CLAIMED YOU LOVED ME. SORRY, WE HAVE NO VACANCIES."

You don't know what I'm talking about? Read the scriptures.

Many will say to me on that day, "Lord, Lord, did we not prophesy in your name, and in your name drive out demons and perform many miracles?" Then I will tell them plainly, "I never knew you. Away from me, you evildoers!" - Matthew 7:22-23

These are not the words of Haman Cross, Jr. Our Lord said them. This scripture is the reason a lot of us don't really believe in hell or think there is a possibility that we can spend (get this) eternity there. ETERNITY! If you are foolish enough to think you can live in hell, you are at least recognizing its existence. But think about this for just a moment: if you are living your life like hell doesn't exist, it's a safe bet that everyone has noticed it, because to do that is to live a life that suggests that God doesn't exist either!

"What do you mean, I doubt the existence of God? How dare you!"

God provides us with concepts of both heaven and hell. Jesus spoke about both places extensively during His ministry, so if you doubt in one, you've probably got some doubts about the other. And before you get too upset about what I just said, think about this: the reason that our testimony to people of the world is suspect is because we are living exactly like we have no idea of who God really is. The world and the enemy are watching us.

Examine yourselves to see whether you are in the faith; test yourselves. Do you not realize that Christ Jesus is in you—unless, of course, you fail the test? - 2 Corinthians 13:5

Whether or not you believe God is real, God does exist. And because God is real, so is hell. If hell doesn't exist, why did Christ spend so much time telling us that it does exist?

My prayer is that you—as they say in the hip-hop vernacular—"don't go there!"

The people that Christ is talking about in Matthew 7:22-23 are people who were doing things "in His name;" people who today would be called "church folk." These were people who were probably telling all of their friends and family about who Christ was and all the things He had done in their life. Let's not forget for one moment that even Satan could tell reports of what Christ did.

Without a doubt, there were people in Jesus' day who thought they were going to heaven because of what they had done "in His name," just as there are people today who think the exact same thing. Have you ever fit into this category, praising God on Sunday and then spending the rest of the week doing Satan's work for him, on your job, with your friends, in your family, in your mind? Do you have a loved one who has lived their life praising God but hating people because of the color of their skin, or their ethnic background? Evangelical Christians of America, black, white, brown, yellow or whatever color you consider yourself, think about that Scripture and examine yourself the next time that you ask the question: "If you died tonight, do you know where you would spend eternity?"

Think about how you or a loved one has lived their life, and ask this question: "if you died tonight, what would the Lord say to you? Would it be...

You hypocrites! Isaiah was right when he prophesied about you: "These people honor me with their lips, but their hearts are far from me. They worship me in vain: their teachings are but rules taught by men." - Matthew 15:7-9

Or...

Woe to you, teachers of the law and Pharisees, you hypocrites!

You are like whitewashed tombs, which look beautiful on the outside but on the inside are full of dead men's bones and everything unclean. - Matthew 23:27

Or would it be...

His master replied, "Well done, good and faithful servant! You have been faithful with a few things; I will put you in charge of many things. Come and share your master's happiness!" - Matthew 25:23

That is a rough road, but we just have to come clean with it all. God is real y'all, so is hell. When I realized that simple fact, and that I didn't want to be one of those "church folk" whom Christ tells plainly, "I never knew you. Away from me, you evildoer," that's when I got real busy doing the work that God put me on this planet for. I got busy bustin' walls in my life.

We need to either admit that we are willing to risk going to hell rather than do the (real tough, hard) things that God wants us to do, or get busy bustin' down walls of partiality. We have to stop being lukewarm Christians. It is time to either make a stand for God or for yourself and ultimately Satan. If you're ready to bust the wall of partiality (and if you've gotten this far through this book, I'm sure you are), then let's begin.

13

❖

How Did Haman Cross the Divide?

"Just as surely as blacks suffer in a white society because they are black, whites benefit because they are white. And if whites have profited from this social structure, they must try to change it. To benefit from domination is to be responsible for it. Merely to keep personally free of the taint of racist attitudes is both illusory and inadequate. Just to go along with a racist social structure, to accept the economic order as it is, just to do one's job within impersonal institutions is to participate in racism."
- Jim Wallis
("America's Original Sin")

"You're looking in someone's eyes, you suddenly realize that this could be the start of something big."
- Ella Fitzgerald

"A racialized society [is] one in which race makes profound differences in experiences, opportunities, and social relationships."
- Emerson/Smith, "Divided by Faith"

Haman Cross, Jr.

We (the Christian Church of America) are living in a highly racialized society and we are also guilty of partiality. Because of the symbiotic relationship of these two issues, we can't deal with one without dealing with the other. Let's not fool ourselves. This is why we have to *Cross Colors*.

It is going to be difficult. I am not going to lie. Crossing colors is at times not only difficult, but it is painful. If it were not, the problem of partiality would have been solved a long time ago. Just as it required Peter to move away from his sin of partiality, it will take the power of God to remove this sin from our churches. It is possible, because God has ordained that we do this. And we will.

Crossing colors requires you to become the two "R's:"

RECKLESS

To *Cross Colors*, we've got to become reckless. That means that you will have to move out of your comfort zone. I don't mean going to a reconciliation-themed event and crying, praying and repenting with someone of another race and then Monday morning, going back to business as usual. That doesn't cost you anything, because at these events there's plenty of emotion. The Holy Spirit has shown up, you're pumped, you're geeked up for Jesus and the ministry of racial reconciliation, and of course you're bothered by the way people of different cultures have treated one another. That's all good. But that guy you were hugging and throwin' all kinds of love on—what was his name? He's not going home with you. You don't have to deal with him at work next week. You'll probably never see him again, will you? Where's the recklessness in that? Guess what? You haven't gained anything because you didn't risk anything.

I'm not asking you to do something superficial. I'm talking about doing something serious! One of the biggest movies of the year 2000 was "Gladiator." Those gladiators put it all on the line. They took risks. At the beginning of the film, before the very first battle, there's a quote that every Christian should memorize and quote before going into this battle.

"What we do in life echoes through eternity!"

Bustin' down the wall of partiality and crossing colors not only feels great and has a profound effect in our own lives, but it will echo through eternity. Just as the sin of slavery has negatively affected generations of Americans that were not born under its pall, bustin' a wall is going to bless generations to come.

Moving out of your comfort zone might mean worshiping at a different church. It could mean attending a different Bible study. It could mean starting your own Bible study where there is a racial mix and where issues are discussed openly, with love, and seeing what God has to say about them. These types of fellowships are very effective in bustin' down walls in not only our lives but in the lives of the people who attend and get involved. They create great opportunities for open and honest communication between people. Getting to know people on a personal level is what helped bust many walls in my life. Opening up the Word of God to hear and experience God through other cultures and perspectives will allow for growth for everyone.

Moving out of your comfort zone could also occur through prayerful, physical, and/or financial support of churches or ministries that focus on *Cross Colors* ministry. Perhaps there is someone in your church who is involved in inner-city missions, or a church that needs financial support or prayer. Get involved! Write a letter. Pray for and with them. Start a prayer group with another church and pray with focus and intentionality to bust walls and *Cross Colors*. Contribute finances to churches that are trying to Cross Colors. You may be the person who needs to begin this kind of ministry in your own church. This goes both ways. Inner-city black churches need to begin to reach out to suburban white churches and vice versa. This is a huge problem and it is going to take huge resources (time, talent and treasure) to defeat it. The Church must bring everything in its power to bear against it.

Moving out of your comfort zone means doing things that your parents probably warned you against. It could mean taking a stand against those who disagree.

Many of the sins in our lives are generational, passed on from parent to child, just as sin was passed throughout our history from Adam. Confronting the way our families have lived their lives is one of the major ways of moving out of a comfort zone, and one of the most important steps in bustin' the walls of partiality.

To *Cross Colors*, we must take on partiality head on—at our jobs, in our churches, in our homes, within our families and within our mind sets. We cannot make a commitment to love someone and continue to tell or laugh at the degrading jokes. Taking partiality head on means that when a relative or friend begins to degrade someone from another culture or background, we no longer ignore it, and we do something about it, especially if this person is calling themselves a Christian. You don't have to be rude or confrontational about it, just speak the truth in love. Let people know that you are a Christian and that acting like a Christian matters to you, because it matters to God.

"Excuse me, but please don't say things like that because it offends me."

"No, I don't find those racist jokes funny at all."

"I'm a Christian and when you say things like that about God's people, you injure them, me, yourself, and God."

We need to let people know that we will no longer tolerate running down or degrading God! That's exactly what we do when we injure others. God created us all in His image and He resides inside each and every one of His creations. If we wound or degrade another person, know that we are wounding and degrading God! Confronting partiality head on simply means taking a stand for God! He sent His Son here to die for our sins. Taking a stand for Him is the least we can do. Just as with every other sin in our lives, we must become intolerant of partiality's presence in our lives. This might mean straining and even changing relationships in our lives, but hasn't every stance you've ever taken for Christ meant this? If it hasn't, you definitely should examine what you have been doing in life and check what Bible you're reading.

For I will give you words and wisdom that none of your adversaries will be able to resist or contradict. You will be betrayed even by parents, brothers, relatives and friends, and they will put some of you to death. All men will hate you because of me. But not a hair of your head will perish. By standing firm you will gain life. - Luke 21:15-19

A friend told me a very powerful story about how his father took a stand against partiality. He told me that when he was younger, his father took him and a few friends to the park to play baseball. On the way, a couple of his friends were in the back of the station wagon "flipping the bird" at people and mouthing racial epithets as they drove past them. As they pulled into the park, his father noticed what they were doing and immediately pulled the car over not far from a man whom the kids in the back seat had insulted. His father made them get out of the car, and they all walked over—his father included—and apologized to the man. He said that he'd always remember that day because his father told them that he was tired of people treating each other wrong.

"My friends were embarrassed and crying while they did it but my old man didn't care. He said that as long as they were going to be around him and his family, he was not going to allow them to grow up to be just another bunch of racist idiots. But when he apologized as well, I realized that he was serious about it. I thought he was just mad because of what they had been doing, but he was actually hurt by it himself. It had a real profound effect on me and my friends to have a parent stand up for what was right. I'll never forget that."

Another way you have to be reckless is by deciding to initiate, develop, and maintain a genuine relationship with someone of another color. I'm not talking about you and the white guy that you work with every day going out and having some beers together. I'm not talking about learning the names of the black couple's kids who live down the street from you, and letting your kids play with their kids. I'm talking about a true, loving and caring relationship; a relationship of Christian love that will be a blessing to both parties involved and anyone else who comes into contact with you.

True friendship is much deeper than just knowing about the person; it's really knowing the individual. It involves trying to understand why they say the things they do, beginning to forgive them if they have offended you, and learning how to apologize when you've offended them.

I'm talking about true discipleship. To disciple someone means to walk alongside them through everything. That's how true, lasting relationships are formed. When you walk with someone, you both develop some dependence and trust in the other, and you will eventually find yourself loving that person. That's why the early church was so strong. That's why miracles happened, because of true love. If you don't have the attributes of love written somewhere on your heart, begin to write them there this very moment.

If I speak in tongues of men and of angels, but have not love, I am only a resounding gong or a clanging cymbal.

If I have the gift of prophecy and can fathom all mysteries and all knowledge, and if I have faith that can move mountains, but have not love, I am nothing.

If I give al I possess to the poor and surrender my body to the flames, but have not love, I gain nothing.

Love is patient, loves is kind. It does not envy, it does not boast, it is not proud. It is not rude, it is not self-seeking, it is not easily angered, it keeps no record of wrongs. Love does not delight in evil but rejoices with the truth. It always protects, always trusts, always hopes, always perseveres.

Love never fails. - 1 Corinthians 13:1-7

Love NEVER fails. Have you ever really internalized the power and truth of that statement? We repeat this bit of scripture often, but how often do we internalize or externalize it? Love, N-E-V-E-R fails! Everything—EVERYTHING—from Genesis 1:1 through Revelation 22:21 hinges on the truth of this scripture! Trust the word of God, children of the Light. That scripture from 1 Corinthians is the scripture that we must have in ALL of our relationships. If you don't intimately know this scripture, you haven't busted many walls in your life. Look over those attributes and understand that they are what you must model in order to move out of your comfort zone and begin new, exciting relationships.

Moving out of your comfort zone may mean developing a relationship that will move beyond friendship and might ultimately lead to marriage, or loving your children enough to support them in one.

Please don't get caught up in the whole ridiculousness and misinterpretation of Scripture about not mixing races. God does not like that! The Bible is clear. We are all one race, one blood.

The bible does not even use the word "race" in reference to people, but does describe all human beings as being of "one blood" (Acts 17:26 KJV). This, of course, emphasizes that we are all related, for all humans are descendants of the first man Adam (1 Corinthians 15:45).

Some people think there must be different "races" of people because there appear to be major differences between various groups, such as skin color and eye shape.

The truth, though, is that these so-called "racial characteristics" are only minor variations among the people groups.

"Scientists have found that if one were to take any two people from anywhere in the world, the basic genetic differences between these two people would typically be around 0.2 percent—even if they came from the same people group. But, these so-called "racial" characteristics that many think are major differences (skin color, eye shape, etc.) account for only 6 percent of this 0.2 percent variation, which amounts to a mere 0.012 percent difference genetically. In other words, the so-called "racial" differences are absolutely trivial." (From One Blood—The Biblical Answer To Racism By Ken Ham, Carl Wieland and Don Batten).

Trust me, nothing breaks down a wall like having a family member standing on the other side. The realization that we are all really ONE race is the equivalent of a nuclear warhead.

It is very hard to look at a grandchild, your own flesh, and decide to hate them because of their color. It's hard to hate people in your own family, although I'm sure there are some people out there who would strongly disagree. This is a very serious way to bust this wall and move out of your comfort zone.

A word to the single Christians of all colors—please don't get caught up in the attitudes of many of your parents that says, "Marry someone from your own race. Marry someone like you. Date within your own race; it's easier." In a sense that is true. You should definitely date and marry someone just like you—a Christian! That should be your number one criteria. Single Christians, I am challenging you to do this—date and marry the person that God wants you to date and marry! There are plenty of Christians who spend their married lives in pain and suffering because they decided to marry someone from their own race, from their own neighborhood, someone just like them. The problem is that many times these are not the people that God intended for them in first place.

I'm going to get off of the subject of crossing colors for just a moment here to make this point. I am not saying that you should go out right now and start looking for someone within a different racial or ethnic background. What I am saying is that if the person that God wants you to marry is a different color, you need to follow God's direction and not society's.

Christians in general need to spend much more time in prayer concerning what is arguably the second most important decision of their lives, behind deciding to ask Christ into their lives, and that's marriage. I can make this statement confidently because of the statistics of the divorce rate among Christians. There are some statistics that show Christians' divorce rate as higher than that of the world's!

When it comes to the area of marriage, don't follow your heart, which is what all the fairy tales, movies and romance novels would tell you to do. Follow God's heart, because this is too important a decision to rely on your own understanding.

Having said all of that, understand that you *should* try to marry someone in your community—the community of faith. Within that community you'll find people of all types of different races, colors and ethnic backgrounds. That is the beauty of Christianity, it is not exclusive: the Body of Jesus Christ is all-inclusive!

For God so loved the world that He gave His one and only Son, that whoever believes in Him shall not perish but have eternal life. - John 3:16

Single Christians and parents of single Christians, if God is bringing someone from our spiritual family into your earthly family, don't get caught up looking at their differences in appearance—look at the similarities of your souls.

That's reckless!

14

❖

How Did Haman Cross the Divide? (v. 2.0)

"You may write me down in history With your bitter, twisted lies, You may trod me in the very dirt But still, like dust, I'll rise. Did you want to see me broken? Bowed head and lowered eyes? Shoulders falling down like teardrops. Weakened by my soulful cries. You may shoot me with your words, You may cut me with your eyes, You may kill me with your hatefulness, But still, like air, I'll rise. Out of the huts of history's shame I rise Up from a past that's rooted in pain I rise I'm a black ocean, leaping and wide, Welling and swelling I bear in the tide. Leaving behind nights of terror and fear I rise Into a daybreak that's wondrously clear I rise Bringing the gifts that my ancestors gave, I am the dream and the hope of the slave. I rise I rise I rise."
- Maya Angelou

The second R is for being **RELENTLESS**.
Relentless (rî-lênt´-lís) adj. 1. Unyielding in severity or strictness; unrelenting. 2. Steady and persistent. (The American Heritage Dictionary)

This is our job as Christians: we do not know when the Lord will return, so we are called to "number our days" (Psalm 90:12). Because of that, we cannot take days off, assuming that Satan is taking days off, because he doesn't. We have to be relentless in our duty.

Let us not become weary in doing good, for at the proper time we will reap a harvest if we do not give up. - Galatians 6:9

One of the ways that we need to be relentless in crossing colors is to build bridges. Bridging the divide; bridging the racial gap; racial reconciliation; Cross Colors, whatever title you use, we must recognize that our inability to successfully negotiate this bridge is problematic for our entire country. It is problematic because this issue is one of the great sins of our country. We must recognize it as sin. If we call it anything else, we will not successfully destroy this sin from among us.

We—Christians—can no longer take the approach of attacking this problem as a social, philosophical, or a secular issue. It is a sin that has haunted, disrupted, handicapped, ruined and ended lives in our country since its beginnings. From the time that Europeans decided to commit genocide on the Native Americans who lived across this land, up until now when we supposedly live in an enlightened society that saw our last presidential election divide right down ethnic and racial lines, we have been and continue to be burdened with this sin.

Let's look at sin.

Sin has been and always will be the wall between God and us. It has separated us from God since the fall of man in the Garden. It was the wall of sin that Jesus— the original wall buster—destroyed when He died on the cross. With the wall of sin knocked down, we now have a way to commune with God. We must be relentless in confronting and dealing with sin.

I am sick of it.

God made me sick of it, and I realize that one of the major calls on my life by the Lord is to bust walls and *Cross Colors*. God has never wanted us to live with sin, but because it is convenient, we will walk, sit and sleep in sin everyday if there is no pressure on us to change. So we must be relentless in destroying the sin in our lives by building bridges.

A bridge is built in order to span a gap; to connect two separate territories together. When Christ suffered and died on that cross two thousand years ago, He was building a bridge for us, between heaven and earth. He was the only Builder who could build such a bridge. When we build bridges, we must not think of them as spans into enemy territory. We are not building a bridge to use to conquer people. That's the kind of bridge building that many Christians have attempted over the years and it ultimately does more harm than good. Many missionaries in Africa, rather than looking at the Africans that they were evangelizing as people with a culture and a soul, thought of them as soulless and inhuman. Because of this, they weren't really building bridges so much as they were dropping bombs in an attempt to destroy their culture. A lot of missionaries in the past and even today are not really sharing the Gospel of Jesus Christ, but trying to change the people into who or what they think they should become.

When we build bridges, we can't have a group on one side of the bridge doing all the work; bringing all their own tools, supplies and equipment, while the group on the other side is busy trying to keep them from building the bridge. Progress would never be made if one group is constantly shooting at the other group, throwing rocks and telling everyone on their side how bad the people on the other side of the bridge are; doing all they can to stop them from coming over. We have got to stop this madness!

We must always keep in mind Whom we serve. Remember, God is the One who is in charge of everything. He has placed everyone where they are, and made everyone who they are for a reason. In our bridge building, we need to realize that the kind of war that we are fighting requires building bridges not into enemy territory, but rather into friendly territory. We are trying to connect two groups of people who are on the same side of the battle.

We are even closer than allies. As Sister Sledge once sang, "WE ARE FAM-MI-LEE!" If we can remember that we are building bridges to meet and get to know family members, then we will have the right mindset for bridge building.

We are building bridges in territory that is owned by the same landowner (God). We are building family bridges. This is a kind of bridge where one part of the family is working on their side, and the other part of the family is working on their side. The object is to span the gap; to meet somewhere near the middle. You don't have to meet exactly in the middle because one group may work faster than the other group.

However, the results are the common bond of spanning the gap.

Working together makes the work easier and shorter. Building the bridge, crossing the divide, or crossing colors requires that we be relentless in doing that.

Another way that we must be relentless is in being intentional.

The book, "Divided by Faith" by Michael O. Emerson and Christian Smith, describes what being intentional looks like:

"Gentlemen," the Promise Keeper speaker bellowed from the podium to a crowd of 60,000 largely evangelical men. "We have grieved our brothers and sisters of color. We have ignored their pain and isolation. We have allowed false divisions to separate us. We must reconcile our differences, and come together in the name of the Almighty God! Turn now to a brother of a different race, confess your sins and the sins of your fathers, and pledge to unite!" All across the expansive domed stadium, small groups formed around men of color. A great murmur of confession rose and reverberated off the stadium top, further amplifying the sounds. Soon, weeping could be heard, first only in pockets, then spreading like an uncontrollable wave, until the entire crowd was shedding tears of lament. "What we have witnessed here, men," the podium speaker said once the sounds began quieting down, "is the power of God's unity. You've tasted it. Now pursue it with a passion! Commit to forming a friendship with a brother of a different race. Be yokefellows, carry each other's burdens, and demonstrate true reconciliation!"

I attended some Promise Keepers meetings just like this one and trust me, that is not only intentional, it is very powerful and cathartic—for the whole family of Christ. America is known and recognized for a lot of things but believe me, the racial divide might well be number one.

One could argue that it is America's original sin. From the genocide and stealing of the land of native Americans, through slavery, segregation, the internment of Japanese Americans during World War II, the Civil Rights Movement, Rodney King, the O.J. Simpson trial, the profiling of Middle Easterners following 9/11, the acquittal of George Zimmerman in the shooting death of Trayvon Martin, the shooting of Mike Brown, to the death of Freddie Gray, race is a constant issue in America.

Partiality is a sin, and we must recognize that it was a sin perpetuated upon people of color, almost exclusively by whites. Because of that, there needs to be repentance. Don't get angry. Don't fall into the trap of saying, "I wasn't even born when all that happened." And don't say the words just to placate someone—we are talking about true repentance here.

The LORD is slow to anger, abounding in love and forgiving sin and rebellion. Yet he does not leave the guilty unpunished; he punishes the children for the sin of the fathers to the third and fourth generation. - Numbers 14:18

Should God then reward you on your terms, when you refuse to repent? You must decide not I; so tell me what you know. - Job 34:33

Repentance is not just feeling sorry for some wrong, or changing your mind about something; it is a turning around or away from something. It is to alter the basic motivation and direction of one's life. The Greek word is *metanoia* and means "to convert" or "to turn around." The history of this country shows a blatant disregard for people who are not of the right European decent (Irish and Italian Americans have been degraded in this country as well). What we are talking about, however, is a more black and white issue. If you are of European American decent and can say that you have never benefited from partiality in this country, you have never practiced partiality, and that none of your forefathers practiced or benefited from it, then I would imagine there would be no need for you to repent. I would also tell you to pinch yourself and wake up. Repentance isn't only about what happened in the past but also what direction you will take in the future.

Repentance is both important and necessary. It is also an incredible testimony and act of trust. By repenting of the sin of partiality, you are telling everyone that not only that are you asking forgiveness for past injustices, but you are proclaiming that you are willing to change the direction of your future and the future of those with whom you will interact. This is not only being intentional but trust me, repentance lays the cornerstone for the bridge that must be built, and it lays a cornerstone on both sides of the divide. The weeping and emotion that takes over Promise Keepers and other reconciliation meetings like those is done by everyone. Everyone gets better. The entire Body of Christ is now beginning to function, as Christ wanted it to, in concert and in focus.

As the old commercial used to say, "Try it! You'll like it!" Being intentional for black people is absolutely vital as well. This is what being intentional looks like:

So watch yourselves. If your brother sins, rebuke him, and if he repents, forgive him. If he sins against you seven times in a day, and seven times comes back to you and says, 'I repent,' forgive him." - Luke 17:3-4

Okay. We forgive y'all. Pretty easy right?

I'm African American, so I'll work from that perspective. Here's my first statement about how we begin to *Cross Colors*:

While African Americans did not create this situation of a racialized society, we are just as guilty of perpetuating it.

"What? Oh, no way! I was with you brother until you said that!"

Brothers and sisters, can we talk?

I would be willing to bet that if you looked at the mission statements of 100 African American churches, you wouldn't find three of them that had as part of their mission to go out and evangelize whites—or any other ethnic group for that matter!

We need to understand that when whites look at African American pastors sharing the pulpit with people who aren't Christian or are claiming to be saved and preaching hate and separatism, they have a legitimate reason for questioning that. How can we move forward if we continue to hold on to our pain and stay in the past? We must make a stand for Christ! We've made stands for everything else. When will we going to start making a stand for our Lord and Savior, Jesus? No matter what you are being told by false prophets, my African American brothers and sisters, there isn't any room between Genesis 1:1 and Revelation 22:21 for Black Nationalism. Trust me, I know because I tried, and it didn't work!

Let me just make it plain. African American Christians NOW HEAR THIS: for all of the injustices, the slavery, the murders, bombings—all of it—we must intentionally forgive white America, just as our Father has forgiven us. I am not asking you to forgive them for their sake. I'm saying forgive them for your sake.

And when you stand praying, if you hold anything against anyone, forgive him, so that your Father in Heaven may forgive you your sins." - Mark 11:25

I urge you, therefore, to reaffirm your love for him. The reason I wrote you was to see if you would stand the test and be obedient in everything. If you forgive anyone, I also forgive him. And what I have forgiven—if there was anything to forgive—I have forgiven in the sight of Christ for your sake, in order that Satan might not outwit us. For we are not unaware of his schemes. - 2 Corinthians 2:8-11

Therefore, as God's chosen people, holy and dearly loved, clothe yourselves with compassion, kindness, humility, gentleness and patience. Bear with each other and forgive whatever grievances you may have against one another. Forgive as the Lord forgave you. - Colossians 3:12-13

Oh, that's a hard one, isn't it? I am not minimizing any of our pain and suffering, trust me I've been there—done that! What I'm saying is that ultimately we have to decide if we will trust what God says or if we will continue to walk by sight and not by faith. This was difficult for me. Listen, there was a time in my life when I could have preached a month long sermon series on why black folks shouldn't trust white folks, especially white Christians. But by leaning on the everlasting arms, I grew up. I didn't stay a baby Christian. And you'd be surprised what God will do for you once you get into this portion of the process. He will put people in your life to walk with you through this—both black and white.

That is a hard one to ask when you look around and still see the things that are taking place, but this is something that we as Christians who are African American must do. When we don't forgive, we are living deep in sin and sin complicates everything.

Therefore I do not run like a man running aimlessly; I do not fight like a man beating the air. No, I beat my body and make it my slave so that after I have preached to others, I myself will not be disqualified for the prize. - 1 Corinthians 9:26-27

For I do not want you to be ignorant of the fact, brothers, that our forefathers were all under the cloud and that they all passed through the sea. They were all baptized into Moses in the cloud and in the sea. They all ate the same spiritual food and drank the same spiritual drink; for they drank from the spiritual rock that ac-

companied them, and that rock was Christ. Nevertheless, God was not pleased with most of them; their bodies were scattered over the desert. -1 Corinthians 10:1-5

When whites reach out to our community and us, when they join our church, we need to return that favor by reaching out to them. We must be intentional in making them feel comfortable and let them know that they are welcome. Don't sit away from them. Greet them like they are a part of your family, because they are.

We, American Christians, should all know that there are people who are caught up in generational curses of partiality. There are literally thousands of families (both black and white) who suffer from this curse. These are the people who for generations have gotten up on Sunday mornings, sung songs, read the Bible and preached sermons, knowing full well that they are holding onto prejudices, stereotypes, and flat out lies. They have never confronted their issues and have passed them down to the next generation.

Some of these people will come into the church to begin to bust a wall and end those generational curses. We can't get so caught up in our own issues that we can't love them with the love of Christ and help them in breaking that curse. Just think about it. If it were a generational curse of excessive anger we'd be there for them, ready right away with counseling. If it were a generational curse of alcohol abuse, we'd enroll them in a program immediately. We must be intentional and ready to do the same thing for someone with the generational curse of partiality! Maybe the Church needs to begin to address the idea of walking with someone that has spent their entire life or grown up in a household that was bigoted. These are the kinds of things that take being intentional to implement and follow through with.

There are people in churches who are constantly saying things like: "Well, this is just the way I am, and they'll just have to deal with it!" You know what I've got to say to that? Maybe it's time for you to change! It's time to grow up and realize that God won't use you the way He wants to if you're sitting there stuck on stupid, and living as if you were born two centuries ago!

Not that I have already obtained all this, or have already been made perfect, but I press on to take hold of that for which Christ Jesus took hold of me. Brothers, I do not consider myself yet to have taken hold of it. But one thing I do: Forgetting what is behind and straining toward what is ahead, I press on toward the goal to win the prize for which God has called me heavenward in Christ Jesus. - Philippians 3:12-14

The only way to confront all of these issues is to become very intentional about crossing colors. We can't be unfocused about this. When people have decided to Cross Colors, they have decided that they are going to do some wall bustin', not only in this earthly realm but that they are going to bust some walls that Satan thought would never be knocked down. Remember, ultimately this is a spiritual battle and Satan has been having his way with us for a very long time. Satan is not going to give up without a fight. He's got his eyes set upon your daughter, your son, and your grandchildren and great grandchildren. If we are not intentional about crossing colors, if we go into this battle without intentionality, Satan is going to be right there with a dump truck full of bricks and a cement mixer so that the walls that God busted will begin to get shored up and rebuilt.

When an evil spirit comes out of a man, it goes through arid places seeking rest and does not find it. Then it says, ' I will return to the house I left.' When it arrives, it finds the house swept clean and put in order. Then it goes and takes seven other spirits more wicked that itself, and they go in and live there. And the final conditions of that man is worse than the first." - Luke 11:24-26

An intentional member of Rosedale explained how he and his family came to our church:

"I had grown up in an inner city, but my wife hadn't. She grew up out in farmland. Her parents were very bigoted. They had problems with me right off the bat because I had no problem with living in the city with blacks, Hispanics, or anybody for that matter. My wife and I met in college doing inner city mission work. That's where our hearts are, so we knew that we were going to eventually become members of an inner city church. A friend of mine from college had heard Pastor Cross preach at college so he suggested Rosedale Park as a church we should visit. Once we visited and heard Pastor Cross, we decided that this was where we should be. We made the decision that we were going to join and that we are going to stay here until God leads us somewhere else, if He ever does. We didn't want to do church hopping or try to find a mostly white or all white church that was doing inner city missions. I know that the only way to get people to give up stereotypes and lies is to show them that people are people and that you can't judge an entire race of people based on a few.

I think a lot of times we forget that the church is like a spiritual hospital, and that in a hospital there are people that are sick and hurting, and that we all have to help them to get better. We've had a few people do some things that I think they did because we are white, but I can't let those kinds of things chase us away. They remind me that I need to pray for them. Those situations have been nothing when I compare them to the friends that we have made. I think Rosedale does a great job at crossing colors mostly because we really take the attitude that we are all one big family, and my family and I are very grateful for our Rosedale family."

Crossing colors will be a challenge for us, but it will be made easier if we submit to God and let Him do the work that we are too complacent and fearful to accomplish.

You will recall Rev. Billy Graham's quote from Chapter 11. "Only when Christ comes again will little white children of Alabama walk hand in hand with little black children." While at first glance this might seem to be a mean and hard-hearted sentiment, Rev. Graham said it not as a rebuttal to Dr. King's speech but as a statement of the hardness of the hearts and minds of the Southerners of that time. It was, at the time, considered a simple statement of fact.

Perhaps this is so, but it does not give any hope, and it certainly does not consider the power of God. It is only through the power of God that we will reconcile, gain the victory and ultimately *Cross Colors*.

15

❖

A Tale of Two Churches

"There ain't no room for the hopeless sinner
Who would hurt all mankind just to save his own
Have pity on those whose chances grow thinner
For there's no hiding place against the Kingdom's throne
So people get ready, there's a train a comin'
You don't need no baggage, you just get on board
All you need is faith to hear the diesels hummin'
Don't need no ticket, you just thank the Lord"
- Curtis Mayfield
("People Get Ready")

In the earlier part of the twentieth century, Fred W. Kanak, a son of Dutch immigrants, decided to start a church. He began holding services, just as the early church did, in his own home. As the congregation outgrew first the living room, and then the converted basement of his home, Mr. Kanak realized that it was time for the church to move to a larger building. Mr. Kanak knew of a man named Mr. Keeger who owned quite a bit of property. Standing in the Keeger home, Mr. Kanak explained to Mr. Keeger that he wanted land for a church. Happy to oblige, Mr. Keeger led Mr. Kanak out his back door, into his cornfield, and began pacing off the land.

"Whoa, hold on there," Mr. Kanak said as he watched Mr. Keeger walk farther and farther out into the corn. *"I only have five dollars."*

"You want to build a church, right?" Mr. Keeger asked.

"Yes, but I only have five dollars to spend on the land," said Mr. Kanak.

"Don't worry about that. You'll need this much land for a church. I want to make sure you've got enough," said Mr. Keeger as he continued to pace off the size of the land he intended to sell Mr. Kanak.

The land he purchased was in what is today called the Brightmoor community, on the west side of Detroit, Michigan. Fred W. Kanak was the first pastor of the church that was first named Brightmoor Bible Church and on February 3, 1936, it opened its doors as West Detroit Baptist Church.

The church grew as the neighborhood grew, catering to its blue-collar white American community. The Brightmoor community was this community even into the latter part of the century. In a city that was devastated throughout the 1950's and 1960's by racial unrest and its byproduct, "White flight." Brightmoor had not really changed that much. It remained a lower to middle class working—mostly white—community. The Brightmoor community had always been in sharp contrast with the community that shared its north and east borders: the upper class and affluent Rosedale Park community.

In the latter part of the twentieth century, I, Haman Cross, Jr., a son of an African American minister, was challenged to start a church. The church was founded with the intention of catering to and helping other African Americans. We began meeting in the living room of my home for a short time as we prepared to actually organize to become the church that we had envisioned. The name of the church was to be Rosedale Park Baptist Church. Although the church was not located in Rosedale Park, we purposed to one day have a facility in that community. The Rosedale Park community has a long history in the city of Detroit. It has always been one of the most affluent communities in the city. In the early 1980's, the complexion of the community had literally changed from an all-white upper class neighborhood to a mixed upper class neighborhood. The vision was that people—black people—who had grown up in the city, received an education and accomplished personal and financial gains, would give back to their community—the black community—through our church. On September 5, 1982, Rosedale Park Baptist Church held its first official service. We weren't yet in Rosedale Park, but we knew that God had plans for our church.

One of the plans that God had for Rosedale Park Baptist Church was for us to *Cross Colors*. This was God's church that He so graciously allowed me to pastor, and this church crossed colors. It wasn't easy, but we made the decision, because this was what God wanted us to do. There was a lot of praying, talking, and tears involved in this transition, yet we crossed colors.

Rosedale Park Baptist was a young church. We had many talented black and white people in our church with plenty of ideas about where God wanted to take us. We were a genuine church family, which was very important for the body of Christ. Then something unexpected happened. The building in which we were worshipping—that had held all of our hopes and dreams—was being sold and the new owners would not be renting the space any longer. We didn't have the finances to purchase the building that we wanted. We came to a huge crossroad in the short history of our church.

Here we were, a growing cross-cultural church and now we didn't know what our future would be. We prayed, we fasted and we prayed some more, waiting for God to show us what He intended for our church. I must admit that I didn't know what would become of us. I couldn't believe that God would forsake us, not after we had changed and begun to *Cross Colors*. I knew here had to be provision for people who wanted to spread the word about God's love and reconciliation as a church in this city of Detroit, a city that is one of the most segregated cities in the United States. Certainly God had a place and a use for a church that wanted to be multicultural, that wanted to *Cross Colors*.

Why would He have brought me this far in my own personal growth, and not provide at least a place for us all to worship together?

We all had come this far by faith, so we continued on in faith, just like Abraham, waiting for that ram in the bush. You see, I knew that God wasn't going to forsake us. The growth and changes that He had accomplished in just my life alone towards racial reconciliation was proof enough for me that He was going to do something for us.

I just had no idea what that "something" would be.

We had service on Sunday, September 8, 1985 for the last time in the building that our church had begun in. I told the congregation to pray for God's provision, for a miracle that would open up a door for our church somewhere.

On the next Monday morning, I went out to have some copies made. I walked into the printing office and as the lady behind the counter began to copy my fliers, we struck up a conversation. I introduced myself and she told me her name was Carol Troast.

"You graduated from William Tyndale College?" she asked.

"Yes, it was Detroit Bible College when I started," I said.

"Do you know Allan Barr?"

"Yeah, I know Dean Barr. I was his basketball coach for a few years! You know him?"

"He's pastor of our church."

"What's the name of your church? Dean Barr used to talk about his church."

"It's West Detroit Baptist Church. What's the name of your church?"

"Rosedale Park Baptist Church."

"Rosedale Park? Where in Rosedale Park is your church? We're right outside of Rosedale Park, in Brightmoor."

"Well, it's not really in Rosedale Park. We started it with the idea that that is where we eventually would like to end up. A few of the members live there and we hopefully intend to move into the neighborhood someday. We're looking to move anywhere at this point. The facility that we've been having services at is being sold, so we're going to be moving."

I didn't want to tell her the whole story.

"You are?"

"Yeah, we are," I said gathering up all of my copies. I still had other things to do that day. *"Tell Dean Barr that Haman Cross said 'Hi' and you have a blessed day."*

"I sure will," she said as I left.

I got a call from Pastor Barr the next day with a proposal that even when I think about it today, almost 30 years later, all I can do is praise God.

Pastor Allan Barr, who was the head pastor of West Detroit Baptist Church, called me up and asked what did I think about a merger of our two churches? This merger would entail me being head pastor, his being assistant pastor and the two churches being merged into one church, Rosedale Park Baptist Church. It would be a mixed church with his church being majority white and ours being majority black, but in his mind we were an answer to a prayer.

West Detroit Baptist Church and the Brightmoor community were feeling the same stresses and strains that the rest of the big cities in this country were feeling in the late 1970's and early 1980's. Urban blight, white flight or urban renewal, whichever catch phrase that you liked, were changing the landscape of the community and the church. Many of the members of the church were moving out of the neighborhood for a number of reasons, and the church membership was dwindling. The members of West Detroit Baptist Church were still committed to the church and the community, which was changing from all white to a mix of black and white. Many of the members who were white wanted to reach out to the black community, but had spotty success. As the size of their membership dwindled, they began praying that God would bring them new leaders and members who could reach out to the community. They already had a building. They just needed people that wanted to *Cross Colors* to fill it!

We were answers to their prayers! They were the answer to our prayers! To make a long story short—God is absolutely great!

Rosedale Park Baptist Church held its first service in its new facility located at 14161 Vaughan in Detroit, MI on September 15, 1985. Two groups of people that who were as different as black and white, night and day, white collar and blue collar had set those differences aside, and let the love of Jesus repair and reconcile those differences. Two of God's churches in America, two different parts of the same body that Christ died for, had come together in His name. Two groups of Christians, who had been sent to each other by God, were bound together in His love. Christians, American Christians, some black and some white, busted walls, crossed colors and worshipped together that Sunday morning back in 1985.

We had church that Sunday morning—we didn't play church—we *had* church, and we've been bustin' walls and crossing colors ever since.

16

❖

THE IDEAL AMERICAN CHURCH

"I know a place
Ain't nobody cryin'
Ain't nobody worried
Ain't no smilin' faces
Lyin' to the races
Help me, come on, come on
Somebody, help me now
I'll take you there"
- The Staples Singers
("I'll Take You There")

Several years ago, I started a church in Detroit. The goal was to begin an African American middle-class church. This was to be a black church that would do some progressive things, not just have car washes, sell rib dinners or build a new edifice on the storefront that we bought. We would be *different*.

As the founding pastor, I was fired up, excited, and pleased about it all. I made it very clear to the Lord and the congregation that there wouldn't be any righteous thing that we would be unwilling to do in fulfilling this vision. We would be *The Ideal African American Church*.

Then God continued a great work on and in my life, the same work that has been going on forever in the lives of His saints. When God placed me in the family of Christ that was made up of all kinds of people with different racial, social, and economic backgrounds, and I was able to *Cross Colors*, He showed me what the Church—His Church—should look like in America: an earthly family.

This idea was well-defined and outlined in our mission statement: The Up and Outers, reaching the Down and Outers. The vision was that people—God's people—who had once been broken and injured by partiality, abuse, the pain and suffering of the world, would give back to the community that we lived in through our church. We would let God's light shine through us and we would be a blessing to our city and our country—even the places we never imagined we would go.

I remain committed to crossing colors and bustin' walls to this day. I can't say I enjoy the pain that often comes as God identifies and confronts my walls, and it hasn't always been easy to *Cross Colors*. But I like what God does in me as the walls come down. I like looking out across our congregation and seeing all the different people who spread and share God's love with me.

Now you know my story.

It's imperative that we heed and share this message. What God wants to accomplish, the walls He wants to bust and the bridges that He wants to build, hinge on our obedience to Him. We must put down the knife of partiality, and help as many people as we can.

Have I arrived? By no means. But I'm committed to going all the way.

Will you go with me?

Epilogue

"A new command I give you: Love one another. As I have loved you, so you must love one another. By this all men will know that you are my disciples, if you love one another."
- John 13:34-35

Haman Cross III, my oldest child, didn't hurt himself that night when he picked up the knife, and he didn't hurt us. I—with the help of our Heavenly Father—finally got him to put down the knife. I remember that night for many reasons. I remember that night every time I look out at the faces of the church that God has allowed me to pastor.

Whenever my grandson, Haman Cross IV, visits Roberta and I at home, I think about the night that his father held on so tightly to the knife. I thank God that He got Haman III to put it down, and that He taught me to put down the knife of partiality as well.

But if you still don't believe my transformation was anything short of miraculous, perhaps this will convince you.

You should know that I wrote the first version of Cross Colors in 2002. It is only recently that I felt compelled to update, self-publish and release it. Now I understand one of the reasons why God needed me to wait.

In Chapter 1, you'll recall that I wrote the following:

Then my children started asking all sorts of questions, the most memorable of which was: "Hey dad, what would you think if one of us married one of the white kids? Would you be mad?"

OHMYGOD!

HOLDUP...WAIT A MINUTE...WAIT ONE MINUTE!

That's why I didn't want them anywhere near our children; they had poisoned their minds already. I was shocked and mortified by the very thought.

I'm not against black folks and white folks getting married or nothing, just as long as the black folks ain't my kids!

My son, Haman III, married a beautiful, godly young woman—perfectly suited for him in every way. It is clear that the Lord has brought them together. They share the same heartbeat for God; for His purpose for them as a couple and in ministry together. God has blessed them with amazing children, my wonderful grandchildren, whom I can't imagine ever having lived without.

Oh, and did I mention?

She's *white*.

Not that it matters to me.

At all.

Pastor Haman Cross, Jr. is Senior Pastor of Rosedale Park Baptist Church in Detroit. A highly sought-after speaker and author nationally and internationally, his hard-hitting and unique style, coupled with his skillful use of humorous anecdotes, enable him to present the word of God in a way that appeals cross-culturally and cross-generationally. His transparency about his personal challenges and recovery has been a source of hope to thousands.

Pastor Cross is available to speak to your group. To request his appearance or to order additional copies of this book, please contact:

Pastor Haman Cross, Jr.
Rosedale Park Baptist Church
14179 Evergreen Road
Detroit, MI 48223
Phone: 313.538.1180
Email: CrossColorsWithMe@gmail.com
Web: www.CrossColorsWithMe.com

❖

Facebook – @HipHopPreacher
@CrossColorsBook

Twitter – @hiphoppreach

Instagram – @HipHopPreach